KICKED IN THE BALLS, AND I AM A WOMAN

Journey to a 140.6

KICKED IN THE BALLS, AND I AM A WOMAN

Journey to a 140.6

Stacy Hughes

ISBN: 979-8-6566-5338-1

Cover design by Andy Meaden / meadencreative.com

To my husband, children & family.

I may be a mess, but I am a *Hot Mess*.

Contents

PREFACE

I started writing this biography five years ago with the intention of documenting my journey towards completing my first 140.6-mile race, otherwise known as an Ironman Triathlon. A 2.4-mile swim. A 112-mile bike ride. A 26.2-mile run. All within a 17-hour time frame. This book is my way of sharing the successes and hardships of competing in one of the hardest races in the world and completing twelve full-distance Ironman events which earned me a legacy spot at the Ironman World Championships in Kona, Hawaii. As my journey continued, my objectives changed and became less clear. Today, the purpose of this project has entirely changed due to an unfortunate circumstance that completely derailed my life. Suddenly, this project has become an opportunity to share with readers the lesson that all is not lost when faced with life-altering events. In fact, life's largest and scariest obstacles often offer us the possibility of reinvention.

I have learned a lot about myself over the last decade, far more than I ever could have imagined. I've grown both emotionally and physically, modifying my priorities along the way. I hope you enjoy my writings and find inspiration that will help guide you on a journey that may not be the clear and precise path you had in mind. Life has no guarantees, and as I've learned, life takes unexpected twists and turns. What seems like clear objectives can be altered. Unexpected change shouldn't break your spirit. Rather it's important to navigate in waters less traveled. That being said, it really is all about the journey rather than the destination. This story has become my coping mechanism and my way of adjusting to the new *me*. This story ends not with the desired original intent, but rather with a new perspective on what is important in my life and how this journey has redefined who I am today. I hope you enjoy it.

"Forever Focus on the Goal" – Stacy Hughes

INTRODUCTION

Life is interesting. I have come to realize over the last five years—and as this journey unfolds—that we as humans are not defined purely by our accomplishments, but by our actions and responses to what life may throw at us. Each human being has their own specific journey, their personality and upbringing shaping their beliefs. The more you explore your individual talents, the more you can help define your goals.

So, a little bit about me: My journey began when I was born in Bridgeport, Connecticut. I was raised with a conservative lifestyle. I could be described as introverted and having a few close friends by my side would allow me to be content. Throughout my youth I was a mediocre athlete. A shy and introverted child, I found team sports difficult and was drawn to individual pursuits, like swimming. In the pool, the only person I could let down was myself. I was very healthy during my childhood and college years. I practiced eating well and exercising daily which I believe is essential to maintaining good balance. At the tender age of twenty-three, I was diagnosed with thyroid cancer. I dealt with treatment, surgery, and a new perspective on life: one that understood it wouldn't always be fair. Spending time in the hospital, I realized I was one of the lucky ones. My health outcome was positive, and I needed to appreciate that I would survive with minimal changes to my lifestyle. As I looked around the hospital and my surroundings, I saw young people and older people who were not as lucky. I quickly learned that neither your ethnicity nor background matter. Sickness does not discriminate. More to come on this topic later.

I continued my education and received both a bachelor's and master's degree in Business Management. I have two children: a girl Bailey, and a boy Kyle. I also have a stepson, Bryant, and a wonderful, supportive husband Daniel. My husband and I balance each other out. As for my children, they are my source of pride. I take joy in their every accomplishment, whether big or small. I have always tried to instill good practices about being active and maintaining a healthy lifestyle. I always encourage them to go on a hike, biking, or joining me for a run (which they tend to gripe or snarl at). Someday I hope they have the opportunity to venture into triathlon sport as well, but regardless it's important to pick a hobby that not only challenges you, but brings passion and happiness. As all people deal with challenges growing up, it's how we respond to them that defines our being. Not all fights are meant to be won, but the willingness to face your fears and challenge yourself is what defines you.

Challenge is something I have always been comfortable with. When I was in my mid-thirties, I was given the opportunity to run a sprint triathlon with a coworker. A sprint triathlon consists of a .5-mile swim, 12-mile bike ride, and a 3.1-mile run. This was the game changer that slowly became my passion. As you read the following chapters, you'll find that my journey and goals evolved. Within the next ten years I had completed the Boston Marathon, numerous half Ironman races, and twelve full Ironman races. During this new journey, around the fifth 140.6-race completion, I set my goals on competing in the Ironman World Championship in Kona, Hawaii. It was going to take twelve full-distance races to earn my legacy spot. This new goal was exciting, thrilling, and extremely challenging. Training nine months a year and racing multiple races each year, for the next six years, was a daunting challenge. I sacrificed a lot of time, energy, and money to become race-ready year in and year out.

As any athlete, I suffered minor bumps and bruises along the way, including a torn meniscus, broken toes, road rashes, and other nuances that came with the sport. I never let these challenges deter me from my end goal of competing in the world championships. Being a modest athlete, I come with average athletic ability. As the years went by, I slowly adapted to the three sports by learning a new lesson from each and every race. With these experiences I was always an athlete who took pride in accomplishing my personal goals.

From the beginning, I chose to document my triathlon journey in a journal with the hope of capturing the events that eventually led to me racing my first 140.6. After lots of online research I sought guidance from fellow athletes in order to understand some of the disciplines that are required to undertake this extreme endurance sport. There are numerous books regarding good practices, but I also found lots of forums that discussed revelations along the way. Online research provided many different resources as to why people decide to take the challenge of completing a full-distance Ironman. Some folks do it as a personal goal, while others train to lose weight, beat an addiction, or prove their disabilities will not be a limitation. Whatever the reason, I hold 100 percent respect for any person who decides to accept the challenge and dedication to the sport. It takes both mental and physical toughness to toe a starting line. Therefore, I chose to document this journal incrementally to include my thoughts and perceptions prior to running the 140.6 race, while also capturing my emotional state all the way up to the first race day.

As you read this, I hope you will gain insight into my thought process, and discover the building blocks that eventually allowed me to embark on a journey to one of the greatest and most difficult athletic events known to mankind: a full-distance Ironman. I learned that there are many aspects to a triathlon and, being a self-taught athlete, I discovered how to deal with injury, nutrition, and mental preparedness (or lack thereof)—both physically and emotionally. This story is about impacts to my family, life balance, and sense of humor. I write this as a story, not as a recommendation; it's about a revelation, a journey that continues, onto a pathway that at this time is still uncertain.

The Journey Begins

Sitting in my cubicle at work, my stomach started to churn. I glanced up at the clock which pointed to 11:48 a.m. It was close enough to start eating lunch. I logged my daily calories, fat, and protein data into a food app, being ever so careful to stay within my daily budget. This was a daily routine occurrence. After having children I had added a few additional pounds to my body résumé. Once work ends for the day, I drive an hour home, change into running clothes, and head out jogging for one to two miles. This was a routine I was comfortable with, it helped me to reduce stress and think about other things in life besides work. On other occasions I would choose to give my body a rest of pounding the pavement and so I would partake in yoga which helps with stretching and flexibility. My daily routine didn't necessarily produce a lean, muscular body, but it allowed me to have my weekend wine and cheese without any guilt.

One afternoon at work, there was a discussion regarding triathlons. It sparked interest. A coworker and I liked the idea and decided to set course and plan a sprint-distance race. I knew I was an avid swimmer in high school, I could run a comfortable ten-minute pace, and how hard could biking be? I had a Huffy growing up that had a banana seat and a basket that could potentially be made aerodynamic if I removed the tassels. So this was my opportunity to venture outside to accept the challenge. Who would ever consider swimming a .5 mile, biking 10 miles, and running a 5K all in one day? I was like Xena, Warrior Princess. If I could accomplish this feat, I would have bragging rights for a lifetime. Some of my coworkers chuckled at the idea, but both my friend and I eagerly signed up for our very first sprint triathlon which would take place in July of 2013.

The first step was to purchase a bike. This was new to me as I never really rode a bike as an adult. So I purchased my first bike from craigslist. It was unfitted and considered a man's bike (but it seems to me that I got a good deal on it). Plus, it was a shiny, greyish-blue color and looked worthy. The bike wasn't expensive and would likely survive the twelve-mile journey of my first race. I rode the bike approximately two times a week and it seemed to do the trick throughout the three months of training ahead of me.

My friends and family didn't understand my eagerness to compete in a triathlon, although they supported my decision. As I explained what was entailed, they suggested I might be entering a midlife crisis and my choices were a direct correlation to not accepting the idea that I was getting older. Or maybe this was my way of proving to myself and others that I was still young, and that age is only a number? Whatever the case may be, I decided to accept the challenge and document what led me to racing. I came to a point in my life when I asked the question "Why not?" This journal would be a good reflection piece and a legacy autobiography for my family.

The time had come and I was ready to embark on my first sprint triathlon: the Appleman Triathlon on July 14, 2013, in Littleton, Massachusetts. The race was about a forty-five-minute drive from my home. The night before the race, I had my gear bag packed with my triathlon suit (to be worn throughout the entire race: tri-top and bottoms), goggles, bike helmet, sunglasses, and sneakers. I felt prepared; I had finished reading many books regarding your first triathlon and used the pre-race checklists to ensure I had everything required to complete this distance. What more was there to do? The night before the race was nerve-racking as people were getting registered and there was nervous energy in the air. I received my swag bag upon registering which consisted of a granola bar, ChapStick, a race bib with my number on it, and a finisher shirt. I didn't want to touch or wear the shirt unless I completed the race and earned the right to sport my swag. That evening we headed over to the pre-race, pasta dinner–event. Of course, we all know that pasta fuels energy, so I would be partaking in a feast for a lion. I mean, really, this was going to be the event of a lifetime, and I wasn't going to be having any shortfalls. So I let loose and carbed up like a senseless woman on a pursuit to accomplish this very daunting feat ahead.

During the carb fest we sat near other veteran athletes—or at least that was my interpretation as they would discuss all of their prior accomplishments. I talked about my nervous energy and concerns. One athlete spoke of the algae-filled lake we would be swimming in, and how I would come out of it covered in muck. She also spoke of how the bike ride would have relentless hills that offered no relief. It took some time to realize that there are people in this world who host negative views or are so ignorant that they have a hard time finding the good in anything or spreading positive vibes. I vowed to never shake another athlete's confidence, especially not a newbie. Triathletes are supposed to encourage fellow athletes and promote a healthy and fun experience. This sport hosts some of the nicest, most supportive people I have ever dealt with.

Race morning arrived and the alarm clock was set for 5 a.m. Instead I woke up at 2 a.m., ready to go. My stomach had butterflies and so I thought that stretching at 3 a.m. might calm the nerves. I quickly learned there is no calming prior to your first ever triathlon and this is the nervous energy we thrive on. My stomach hurt as the overly intense carb-loading the night before may not have been as forcefully required. I managed to muster a small breakfast consisting of a bagel and coffee. At 5:30 a.m. I was pumping up my bike tires, placed the bike in the car, filled my water bottles, threw my triathlon bag in the car, and off we went. Arriving at the race at 6:15 a.m. was electric. You could see a lot of nervous, excited energy. I racked my bike according to my bib number, set up a staging area next to the bike for the transition from the bike to the run, and then proceeded to head towards the lake with goggles and swim cap in hand.

My swim heat was finally up, and I was wading in the water with a bunch of women in bright pink caps. We had all been blatantly marked with our age written with an extra thick sharpie across the calf. It seemed odd as the ages ranged from eighteen to seventy and over. The playing field was open to anyone. I considered my age-marking on the back of my calf as a badge of honor. Here I was, almost forty years old, getting ready to embark on the same journey as everyone else and this was my opportunity to embrace competition. Granted, it was odd when the gun went off, to look out on the lake with each wave taking off and seeing masses of heads bobbing up and down in different colored caps—it was like watching a rainbow of skittles all afloat.

The lake water was chilly but refreshing. The swim wave of ladies in my age group was smaller, which made it easy to find my own space in the water. Concentrating on staying calm and reminding myself that *I got this* was exhilarating. Upon nearing completion of the swim, I saw the shoreline approach, and I stood up to run under the swim FINISH banner. I had made it, my swim was complete—not boast worthy by any means—but in my eyes a success. I was unaware of where I finished the swim compared to the others in my age group, but I was not worried because this was about my personal goal. I ran to T1 (first transition to suit up for the bike ride) and grabbed my bike. I put on my helmet and ran to the start line, bike in tow. My helmet was riding on my head backwards. Oy, my rush to the start line had impaired my good judgment. I mounted my bike and was proud of it. It was a decent-looking road bike, and it didn't have a horn attached or a side mirror so all was good. I saw my husband and children smiling. My husband had purchased a funny-sounding cowbell from one of the vendors on-site, and I could spot him a mile away. I basked in the enjoyment, hearing my mom and children hooting and hollering, and this was my moment. I had a smile across my face from one ear to the other. I was in my element, feeling primed, excited, and supported. I reached the start line and headed for the hills. I jumped on my bike and ferociously pedaled towards the sunrise. Instantly I heard a rotation with a tug, and looking down I came to the realization that my chain was off my bike and I was quickly and abruptly stopped. Nothing had prepared me for this. Saddened I watched people fly past me as I tried to flip my bike over with my family members looking on in disbelief, knowing I was alone and needed to get it together and fix it myself. Never had I worked on a bike, changed a flat, or addressed any issues. This was a scary thought. I quickly flipped my bike over and luckily my inkling was right; as I rolled the tire and picked up the chain, it caught, and I was once again on my way. Ego slightly damaged, but on my way. A mile up the hill I changed gears and dropped my chain again. I rode the remainder of the race in a high gear, looking slightly odd pedaling up hills standing, just to keep the bike in motion.

Ahh, the bike portion was complete, yes! Time was not a concern. My only goal was to finish the run. I had hoped to average a ten-minute mile which is exactly what I achieved, no record breakers. With the run complete I eagerly listened to my family's cheers as I crossed the finish line and heard my name announced: "Stacy, you are an Appleman." With my ego in hand, my smile took nearly a day to relax. I went home and slept. I was exhausted. I committed, conquered, and completed a triathlon. My competitiveness was seeping through. This race triggered and fueled a new passion for future triathlons.

Conquering New Territory

My next triathlon was set for the fall of 2013. It was an all-women's race in Hopkinton, Massachusetts, called Title 9. This was a unique race because it shares some of the same running course as the Boston Marathon which is near and dear to me. Being a lifelong New Englander, I always considered it a special race and I was envious of all the athletes who had the opportunity to run it. It brought forward some of the best running athletes in the world and was a bucket-list item I would pursue one day. As with each race an athlete chooses, it becomes a lot of fun trying a new course with uncharted territory. The Title

9 triathlon, on September 8, 2013 was an example of that. It was for sure another memorable race as well, since this was my first women-only race. It was an opportunity for kinship. We were all on this journey together and offered each other encouragement. The race had a great reputation for athlete support and inspiring women to be successful. We all shared the same adrenaline rush and nerves around what was to come during the race. This was one of the few races that went very smoothly for me. The swim was in a crisp, clear lake and the bicycle ride was just enough rollers to be challenging but not overwhelming. The run was full of spectators enthusiastically cheering you on therefore, making it unforgettable and very enjoyable.

Winter of 2013 came and I relied on living room workout videos in a commitment to keep up my current level of fitness. As the new year rolled around, I scoured a triathlon website eager to find my next great challenge. I ended up registering for the same triathlons as I had the previous year, including the Appleman and Title 9, seeing it as an opportunity to benchmark my progress. I was happy about my progression over the year as with each race I saw improvements on my times. The swims became minutes faster, the bike rides went from 15 mph to at times 19 mph, and the running times would average in the eight-minute range.

In 2014, I completed half a dozen sprint triathlons and Olympic distances. An Olympic-distance triathlon consists of a .93-mile swim, 24.8-mile bike ride, and 6.2 mile run. Both the sprint and Olympic distances became a real enjoyment. Knowing I would never be elite, I was content with my performance and just wanted to continue improving while pushing myself out of my comfort level. I craved to run a quicker mile and shorten my overall race times. I was committed to self-satisfying goals. I had worked hard over the years and my children and husband would continue to watch my triathlons and were always excited and full of encouragement. My hopes were to always inspire my children and set a good example for them. Goals are essential and required to stay motivated.

I was ready to take my triathlon passion to the next level and therefore investigated the opportunity to compete in a half Ironman. This distance intrigued me. The race is a total of 70.3 miles which consist of a 1.2-mile swim, 56-mile bike ride, and 13.1-mile run. What a challenge to take on—one I was willingly ready to accept. The first thing I did was run to the bookstore to buy a 70.3 training book, a marathon-running book, and a nutrition guide. This would be the ideal start. As an anxious athlete I picked a newbie training plan, ordered triathlon magazines, and subscribed to a club for athlete snack boxes to be delivered monthly to the house. This would be a great way to introduce my body to new gels, granola bars, protein packs, and some other odd snacks, including cricket powders. *Interesting*. My thought was that my palate should be developed further to introduce new foods (mostly carbs). I also had the ability to find different ways to add more protein to my diet, to help build muscle post-workouts. Most importantly, it was imperative to find out what snacks my body would tolerate to help get me through race day. When training for a sprint triathlon it was fun eating jelly bean carbs (almost a treat), but at greater race distances the idea of eating jelly beans every fifteen minutes for seven plus hours sounded repulsive.

Longer-distance athletes need to accommodate their nutrition to the race conditions. It is imperative to be as race-ready as possible given the environment and time of year of the race. The swim can be chilly or warm, choppy or calm. The bike and run can be windy, hot, cold, flat, or hilly. The day can start out beautiful and then take a turn midday. All of these environmental shifts can change your fueling strategy. You are more likely to burn an increased amount of salt sweating on a ninety-degree day versus when it is sixty degrees and raining. Considerations need to be made for fluid intake and the amount of carbs required to complete the race. All of these nutrition considerations should be worked out to the best of your ability prior to race day to ensure a healthy race and to lower your chances of having gastrointestinal (GI) issues. As they say, ten miles into a run, never trust a fart. Nutrition and fluids are critical to securing a successful race. Also watching the weather report like a hawk ten days out from the race becomes a triathlete's focus—almost a compulsive reflex.

I started training for Rev3 Quassy in Middlebury, Connecticut—now known as the Ironman 70.3—which would take place on June 1, 2014. Of course, we all make rookie mistakes and the expression "too much, too soon" that we all read about in magazines and books would prove a little too accurate during my preparation. As training progressed, my coworkers coerced me into signing up for a half marathon to be completed a week prior to the 70.3 triathlon. It seemed like reasonable preparation to help get my distance up to thirteen miles, allowing me to be ready to embark on the tri race a week later. Without proper training I found myself very aggressive with the running. Of course, running with your working peers will do that, as ego once again plays a big role in encouraging bad behavior. I was clipping at an eight-minute mile while also jumping on the bike for four-hour rides right out of the gate. I felt unstoppable until that dreaded moment on a long ride when I felt a rub, almost a tear, and the pain was immense. The back of my knee and the side of the patella felt wrong. Not really understanding the ramifications, I pushed through the pain to acquire the mileage I was determined to hit that day. I had goals and this was nothing Advil or ice couldn't fix. RICE, I'd read, was the way to go. Rest, Ice, Compression, and Elevation. After a week of feeling sorry for myself and cutting back my running mileage I saw a doctor. This was when I was told about the torn meniscus in both knees along with a Baker's cyst. Foam rolling and wall squats were about to become my new best friends.

As race day eventually approached, pain management was under control—to a degree. The underlying issue remained. I could now get to nine miles without pain before the patella would fatigue and the kneecap would start skipping like an 8-track tape. Knee braces were something I invested in. I now had a drawer full of contraptions that included KT Tape, gels, brackets, Velcro, and straps for knee support. I tried them all in the search for a miracle fix.

Race day was here. I had arrived in Middlebury, Connecticut, at the Rev3. The race started next to an amusement park which looked like a fun way to spend the post-race afternoon. The excitement was more than I could handle. The weather was perfect and the swim looked to be unintimidating. You could see markers in the water guiding your direction. The swim didn't look all that long, but I was sure it was visually deceiving. The bike ride was described as very challenging, with over 4,000 feet of climbing within the fifty-six miles, and the run would take place throughout the rolling hills of Connecticut.

I stood at the start of the swim line in a sea of green neoprene swim caps. The adrenaline spiked as our heat was told we were up next. I glanced at my husband who stood there with the same cowbell from the very first race. It was a sound I had grown so familiar with. I could search a crowd of hundreds of people and pick him out on a dime, it was very comforting. The family was waving, and I felt a sense of pride. I was ready to embark on this journey to gain the 70.3 medal.

The gun went off. I ran in full excitement and launched myself into the lake. The water hit me like a polar plunge. My wetsuit grabbed me in a vice grip over my chest and my alarmed breathing pattern turned into straight panic. *I want out!* I was fifty feet into the water and I couldn't breathe. I had come all this way and fear had suddenly turned me into a woman who needed to shed the armor that was sucking the wind from her chest. I repeated this mantra to myself: *I can't quit, it's not in me*. With the little self-control I could muster, I unzipped the back of my wetsuit and unfolded it to my waist. I flipped onto my back and looked up at the sky while trying to recompose rational thinking. I tried to overcome the thoughts of telling my friends, family, and coworkers that two minutes into the race I had quit. I was not a quitter. What felt like a lifetime within this moment was probably closer to five minutes. I calmed my thoughts, flipped over onto my stomach and made way with my wetsuit dragging behind me, creating an awful drag. That was the least of my concerns. I was not going to be defeated. I was going to regain control and complete this, and that is what I did. Being self-taught triathletes, we learn from each race we partake in. This race was full of rookie mistakes. Life is about growing and evolving. I had trained according to a plan, but never thought about testing the equipment prior to the race. With most races I had competed in, the swim was short and the water temperature was comfortable enough to wear a tri suit. Of course, these were always sprint or Olympic distances. I had jumped from a smaller race event to a "no kidding, you need to bring your A game if you want to complete this"-race. I was an accomplished scuba diver and wetsuits were a given, so I went with the thought that the extra buoyancy and added warmth were nothing more than a plus on the day of the triathlon. I never anticipated the shock of the cold water, the tightness of the wetsuit, nor the adrenaline rush that would consume me that day. I eventually regained my self-control, although the drag from wearing the wetsuit waist-high was like having a mask on a sailboat, and I managed to finish. Short of a few tears, I was super excited to see my family waiting to greet me and watch as I headed off to the transition area prior to the bike portion. I also needed to shake off my dismay and erase any negative thoughts regarding the swim. The next part of the race was going to be a challenging fifty-six-mile bike ride ahead. I mustered my thoughts for the next task at hand.

It was a gorgeous summer day and the bike course had been likened to rolling hills, while I would describe it as equivalent to the Superman roller coaster at Six Flags. All went well until mile twenty, when I heard a rumbling sound that I hoped was just a ridge in the road. I pulled off to the side and checked my tires. I had indeed incurred a flat on the back tire. Now, you probably would've thought that after my first sprint triathlon experience I would have subscribed to *Bike Mechanics Weekly*. Well, I'd taken triathlon training much more seriously at this point, and I was committed to practicing tire changes and basic mechanical issues. But as I flipped my bike over, I soon realized my brain was in complete race mode and not mechanic mode. This made it difficult to address the issue with a clear mind. Watching flocks of bikers fly past me was intimidating and discouraging. I realized it was a hard transition to become technically inclined under stress. Fortunately, the road-side crew and the voluntary helpers were in the area and available. This is a first come, first served–process. This is the only reason race day was so successful for me. Volunteers don't get enough credit. They are the unsung heroes during a race and are the linchpin to a successful race. The support crew assist all competitors hour after hour through whatever weather conditions Mother Nature chooses to throw at us. I kindly ask all triathletes to remember to always thank the volunteers during race day. They are supportive and kind people who donate their free time to all athletes. Therefore, they should feel appreciated throughout the day. Please always remind yourself to be kind and offer a thankful shout-out to as many folks as you can. The race volunteer I dealt with was able to calm my nerves; as he tended to my tire he reminded me that this was a great opportunity to take on extra fluid and stretch out my legs. He offered kind words of encouragement and before long I was on the bike and back in the race again. The extra fluid and break off the bike actually gave me a new adrenaline rush. My legs felt fresh and ready to continue forward. Later in the race around mile forty-five, the bike support crew made their rounds again and as they did I heard “Stacy, woohooo, go get it!” My volunteer had spotted me and, again, he eagerly shouted amazing words of encouragement and it made me feel like a million bucks!

The run was very demanding and my legs felt fatigued. The hills had definitely challenged my well-being. On some of the steeper climbs I was forced to walk. Along the route I met an older gentleman who gave me a pep talk and also asked when I would be signing up for a full Ironman. To this I replied, "That will never be on my radar." At that point I was feeling the pain in my knees and joints, and my running gait was being challenged. He mentioned this new concept to me called the RWR (run-walk-run method). He spoke about how changing between the running and walking allowed adequate recovery for your body, and that it helped correct your running form in order to reduce the risk of injury. I nodded at the idea and quickly dismissed the proposal in my head. The notion of racing 140.6 miles made my head spin. I could calculate the distance as leaving my house in Massachusetts and nearly making it to New York City all on my own devices. This was not a challenge even worth consideration. He went on to also recommend that I investigate competing in Ironman Lake Placid, since it was so serene and rather close to Connecticut. I thanked him for the pleasant conversation and trotted off.

The day rolled on and the running race was exciting. There was a fair number of spectators along the course eagerly cheering us all on. Finishing this race was a feather in my cap. My times weren't record breakers, but I had accomplished the goals I'd set for myself. I also took this as a chance for learning and checked the box that I'd completed a 70.3 race. I thought to myself how proud I was of what I had just accomplished. This was such a significant feat and I knew without a doubt that I was bound to find a new journey to embark on next year. The thought of getting stronger with each race and the opportunity to improve my times were an incentive that had me hooked. I was intrigued with the newfound idea of each race achieving a new personal record (PR). This was the reason I chose to continue racing.

For the remainder of 2014, I decided to give myself some well-needed rest from triathlons. My body ached and allowing it to recover properly was required. Therefore, for the rest of the summer and fall I focused on local shorter-distance running races. This was my chance to participate in some fun runs with my kids, including the local Taco Run. This race took place on a local high-school track, and was designed as a relay race. I decided to embrace this opportunity with my reluctant daughter. I started off the race by eating a full burrito, after which I had to run 400 meters and pass the baton to my daughter, who would then also need to consume a burrito prior to running 400 meters. Going back and forth we both ate four burritos each and swore we would never again partake in any sort of race that required consumption of Mexican food.

We also tried a 5K color run which was by far amusing. Both my kids embraced this concept. The idea was to wear white shirts. We were then handed a ziplock bag of pastel-colored powder and were encouraged to throw the chalky substance at participants throughout the run. By completion of the race you would have an array of colors all over your outfit. At every half mile we were given an additional bag with different colors. What we weren't prepared for was the fact that it was going to be a rainy day. As our hands were wet, we reached into the bags which now held clumps of colored chalk. When we tried throwing it at each other, we were launching balls like from a Nerf gun—it was pretty amusing. We approached the finish line with the same white shirts, except they had taken some direct color hits as if we'd been playing paintball.

Of course, we needed to finish the running season with a Zombie 5K. This was an eerie race that the kids were a little skeptical about. The course took us through a cemetery and down a road covered by trees that hung over on both sides. Around the 2.5-mile range, nearing the finish line, the zombies were laying on the ground, dragging themselves by their elbows and moaning. Some of them walked out from behind trees—it was both fun and frightening. At that point my kids decided they did not want to proceed with the race and begged to turn around and head back. After some coercing and explaining that we were over three-quarters through the race, they obliged and maneuvered around the questionable-looking zombies, and completed the race clearly stating that they would never partake in that again.

The 2014 racing season was over. It was fun to incorporate both triathlons along with a mix of unique running races. Over the winter it was important to learn from all of my quasi mishaps during training. These lessons would be valuable as building blocks for future races. I strived to become a more informed, self-sufficient athlete. You can read book after book, but each hand of circumstances an athlete is dealt is unique and has the potential to become a stepping stone to growing your confidence. How you handle yourself in any given situation also builds self-awareness. Overcoming the unknown, or being unprepared for the worst, is what builds your character and belief in your abilities going forward. All races create unique scenarios. The most well-built plan along with a perfectly executed race is unlikely in the triathlon sport. I have heard countless stories over the years when talking with fellow athletes. Once I met a man during the run portion. He was distraught. He had forgotten his socks at home and discovered his mistake while transitioning over to the run. He was an excellent runner but his feet were torn up from the friction of his sneakers. There was another time when I saw a woman bleeding from all of the chafing burns on her legs and arms. After these two circumstances, I am sure the man never again forgot to double-check his race bag to ensure all essential race gear was protected, and that the woman would research solutions to prevent chafing. These are some of the examples from other folks that also helped me evolve in the sport as well.

Fall was quickly vanishing and winter was inbound. The leaves had started their departure from the trees. I had nurtured my wounded knees and shared my experiences with my family and friends. My year-long goals were met, and I was on a quest to seek a new adventure. One evening, my husband and I were playing a round of poker with friends, as we occasionally did. The conversation of the rehabilitation of my knees came up, and I gestured that I could check off completing an Ironman race. My husband corrected me by saying I had only finished “a half Ironman.” The remark was like the shot heard around the world—or at least by the six people around the table. This fueled the fire. A spark went off that I was not going to be remembered for only doing “a half.” I am always in it for all or nothing.

After reading numerous blogs on running and triathlons, I learned you would never say that you completed a marathon if it was truly only a half. I am not demoralizing half marathons, a feat few people are daring enough to do. But there is a difference between crossing the threshold of 13.1 and 26.2. So how could I quantify a 70.3 the same as a 140.6? I knew, at that point, what needed to be done.

Training Commences

November 2014 rolled in, and I was on a quest to accomplish a full-distance 140.6 Ironman race. This new journey sounded so appealing and challenging. If I were going to go all out, I would want it to be in a location that sounded tempting. I wanted a race that I wouldn't have to wait nine months for. Being an impatient person, I was in need of results. I sought goals and reasons to be motivated. That's when Ironman Texas 2015 presented itself in a cloud of mystery. A nice hot location and a state I'd never explored in the past. A time of year I could readily train myself and be ready for. This was my time, my opportunity to live the dream. Without a whole lot of thought—and a couple glasses of wine—I invested in the challenge. I paid the dues and booked the flights, hotel, and bike transportation. I was committed.

Back to the bookstores. I needed a plan. I purchased a beginner's 140.6 training plan. I didn't want my training to lead to an injury and my goal was to complete the race within the seventeen-hour time constraint. I had read along the way that there is a multitude of athletes who have committed to the challenge of balancing family, work, education, house, sports, etc., and are still dedicated to the hard work of completing this daunting task. As any working parent with children knows, time management is essential. Different training plans indicated that a beginner Ironman-triathlete should plan on six to ten hours a week in the first half of the training plan and up to fifteen hours in the remainder. This seemed daunting. The thought was for sure intimidating. I didn't feel as though I had that amount of time free from my current life, so how was I going to find an extra ten to fifteen hours a week to accommodate this new journey? The mere idea seemed overwhelming at times. I decided to manage my new training load day by day. Looking at the picture as a whole would be too overpowering. Looking at each day separately I could conquer the task. Bite-size pieces were more feasible than eating the entire cow in one serving.

Every athlete's perception of training is different. Some athletes have the ability to achieve a sub-twelve-hour race. For me, I needed to balance all of my personal circumstances. I decided early on that I would dedicate the amount of time that my schedule allowed, and I prepared as well as I could. Personally, I believe it's about finding balance, harmony, and the discipline to commit to the challenge. Granted, there's the occasional hardcore athlete whose body can perform in ways I will never be able to comprehend. The elites of our sport continue to fascinate me. Their athletic capacity is mind-blowing and I am beyond envious. But my story is that of an athlete dedicated to challenging my drive, self-motivation, and commitment to the sport at my level. My goals are independent of every single person who attempts this challenge. My objectives are based on my personal situation, my day-to-day activities, and, most importantly, my family. This ultimately will always be most important to me. My pride has always been watching my children evolve and grow up to become mature, accomplished adults. Although racing is a massive part of my life I never want to lose sight of this. I am also incredibly invested in my career and spending time with my husband. We share many passions together, like scuba-diving trips, playing golf, or having a glass of wine at home in front of the TV. This is my primary focus in life. My triathlon goals are a subset and it is important to find a happy medium between all of it. I am fortunate that my family chose to support my goals as well. They have encouraged me day in and day out, and have embraced my choices.

I began training during the winter of 2014–2015 for my first full-distance Ironman in The Woodlands, Texas. The goal was to complete training in six months to be worthy to compete in May 2015. November was the pivotal time when I embraced a training plan. A set schedule was developed, one that would dictate my daily life for the next six months and which I must maneuver, manipulate, and create time for. What my training plan did not account for was a winter in Massachusetts. A winter like no other, one that would go down as the snowiest winter on record. I needed a plan that would encompass my geographical situation. Signing up for a race in Texas during the spring was going to be a challenge since my geographic location would never allow me to simulate the same conditions.

The transition started. The living room chair had been moved to the basement, the spinning bike to the living room, and the treadmill to the basement. The bedroom was a cluster of yoga mats, foam rollers, weights, sneakers, and a dresser full of workout clothes. I believe you know you have embarked on this journey when you realize that every load of laundry contains dozens of workout outfits and towels from the pool. My dresser had become loaded with KT Tape, books, printouts, Advil, GPS watches—an array of equipment to make me more effective and efficient.

The training plan throughout the winter was manageable. I found ways of spending time with the kids, reading books while biking, and incorporating yoga stretching with them. I also took them to the pool on Saturdays during open/lap swim. We watched movies together while I biked for hours and hours at a clip. Training in Massachusetts is tough over the winter. The weather is unforgiving and being house- and gym-bound can be daunting. I needed to be on paved roads and have the ability to go on a quest to venture into new areas on my bike and on my runs. I wanted to feel the heat on my face and place my cold gear in a bin, far away from society on a planet in another galaxy. Running on a treadmill for two and a half hours in the basement or biking for four hours in the living room is mentally draining and also unrealistic to actual race conditions. Therefore, I decided my end goal should be to just stay driven and keep my eyes focused on the prize.

As the plan continued to build, my body was feeling the tension. My knees hurt and my back and neck singed from time to time. The long bike rides sitting in an aerodynamic position for hours at a time were difficult. This aggressive position recruits many muscles to be engaged and weaknesses in those muscles would likely present themselves. Sometimes after getting off the bike, my toes would cramp to a point that they would bend like an L. I would call my children into the room for the quick gross-out factor. My restless legs stirred in the middle of the night. My body ached from the repetition. Ice, stretching, massages, and frequent appointments to my physical therapist throughout the winter became routine.

One day I decided to embrace the beautiful, glistening snow that had graced our town almost on a daily basis. Over nine feet of snow fell that year, a record. As an athlete this was my opportunity to mask my pain in my first ever ice bath. Embarrassed by the idea of plunging my barely dressed body with just running shorts and a t-shirt on, I had invited my daughter to share such a joyous occasion. I opened the front door for the first time on that brisk February morning and without thought I leapt like a deer into the snow. Yikes, who knew how shocking this would be? My daughter giggled as she scooped snow into her pink little hands and rubbed my knees. She continued to scoop piles of the heavy snow all over my legs until they were covered. I shrieked, pulling my toes from the voyage that the rest of my body was taking. It was a painful ordeal. After what felt like an eternity—but was only around five minutes—I ran back into the warm house and let the snow fall off me into a dripping puddle of slop. Wow, how invigorating it actually was! My legs gleamed red but they now felt like they'd been reprised in the body of a twenty-year-old. I was energized and felt empowered on my journey. As the months passed, I made this a ritual every couple of weeks. It was a pick-me-up for a deflated, aching body.

The planned workouts became more demanding of my time and body, and I became increasingly edgy about venturing out on the roads again. I was stir-crazy and wanted to feel the tar under my feet and the bumps in the road. I wanted to ride off into the distance. Desperate for fresh air and the freedom of the great outdoors—but knowing that my road bike can't take the New England road conditions with the road salt, snow, and potholes—I decided to take my young son's mountain bike off for a journey. Looking like a bear on a tricycle, I rode ten miles with brakes that worked by pedaling backwards. I'd accepted the voyage of an athlete at all costs. I got lots of interesting stares, which I shooed off with the thought of my end goal in mind. I was desperate for the outdoors and as months passed, I found other ways to cope with the cold and complete my mission.

With lots of other athletes, I had hit a slump and I am sure I was irritable at times. I would come home snappy and short-tempered considering the conditions and temperatures I had to deal with. I would have tears in my eyes as my toes burned in discomfort from running in the cold, and my fingers felt the bite of winter. This is truly when I needed a supportive spouse the most, and my husband was well-versed and understanding of my dismay at the situation. I was always encouraged by my husband to share my woes, pains, twinges, discomforts, etc. He was and still is there for me every day. I have been consumed by workouts, nutrition, and balance of schedule, but I have never once been faced with a man who made me feel like I made a bad decision. He became a rock for me. Not a day has gone by without discussion of training or the big race. I am sure the monotony of the daily routine could make a person go mad, but I've learned that the love, support, and commitment of my family are what made this possible. Without them I would not have the drive, motivation, or feel the need to commit as heavily as I did and still do.

Spring finally arrived. Although there were still extremely cold days, every so often I would be treated to a day where temperatures reached forty-two degrees. What a delight! Having the ability to head outside for fresh air was very welcomed. At this point, training commenced in a variety of mixed formats—some inside, some outside. The new diversity in my workouts became a real treat.

As I was barreling through the training plan, spring was in full force. The snow had melted, which was a relief, and my snow-angel retreats had subsided into thin air. During one outing I completed a long run and became sore. I grabbed my ice packs, my two children, and snuggled in for a movie. I pulled the blanket up and basked in their hugs and affection. The movie ended and to my horror I had left the ice packs (yes, placed directly against my skin as noted on the package never to do) on my knees and forgotten their presence. My kneecaps were awful. They looked as though they'd touched down onto a plate of hot coal. I met with an orthopedist only to be told that I had a touch of frostbite on both knees. My knees transitioned from weeks of red and purple to peeling dead skin. Yes, another mistake. I had opted to help muscle recovery and reduce swelling by being overly proactive, and instead I had to enjoy watching my knees change color like a mood ring.

People often ask whether I ride or run with anyone. Doesn't being part of a group provide you with additional motivation? My answer to the first question is no. I do not usually run with partners because I enjoy the peace and quiet when taking in my surroundings, it is almost like meditation. It's my time to mentally unwind and contemplate everything that is currently on my plate, or to think about nothing and just enjoy nature; taking in the wildlife, listening to the birds, and even watching people do yard work and tend to their gardens. Basically, absorb it all.

I also like to pace my run to what is comfortable for me. I have tried numerous times in the past to invite or join other runners, but, quite honestly, the pace always seems either too fast or too slow. I like to call the shots and set out based on how I am feeling. I understand that people motivate others and can help you run upwards of 10 percent faster, but my focus is on relying on my own body's instincts. I also like to set the course based on my day-to-day interests. Because my life is chaotic with children in school, and work, I try to fit my workouts in based on time constraints. I am lucky enough to have a job where the leadership supports my efforts, and, therefore, allows longer lunches to accommodate lunchtime swims. I sometimes wait until later in the day to run in order to have extra warmth and daylight. I also bike on the weekends when my kids are occupied with other interests or still asleep in bed. I stay committed to my daily workouts, but the time of the day would vary by the week to accommodate my typically busy schedule.

I took my training to a personal level in which I was satisfied by completing my goals and maintaining a pace that was comfortable to me. The few times I did join a group on a ride was fun. Group riding is different because you are allowed to draft. Drafting can allow a rider the advantage of becoming almost 20 percent more efficient when placed in the middle of the pack. While drafting in triathlon is against the rules, if caught you could suffer a five-minute penalty added to your time. If done more than two times you are disqualified from the race. That being said, riding with a group on the weekend was fun because you got to reap the benefits of having much faster times than riding alone. The group-ride results were always a great ego booster. However, I still mostly enjoyed riding alone and seeing self-improvements in training times when left to my own devices.

Reflections

Training for a 140.6 race requires pure devotion and love of the sport. From fitting in two swims, runs, and rides a week, to weight training, yoga, and other forms of exercise in order to help train your muscles, there was little time to rest. As the miles started to stack up and training was averaging ten to fifteen hours a week, my knees as usual started to act up. This was a time when intervention had to come into play. Visits to physical therapy became routine; massages were bi-weekly; icing, rolling, stretching, and core strengthening became critical players in my training. I realized I had hit a point where my body was responding to the impacts of prolonged training. Therefore, I once again headed to the bookstore to research injuries, remedies, and different training options. I always questioned my ability to run twenty-six miles after biking such a long distance, and I remembered that man's advice during my first 70.3 race, which was to try the run-walk-run (RWR) method. As I read more on this topic, I decided to give it a shot. My intentions of going into the race would be a one-minute walk and a four-minute run. This would occur every time my watch hit a five and nine. With the race only weeks away at that point, I could only hope that my preparation would keep me injury-free and ready to go. Prior to using the run-walk-run method, the pain I endured was not only frustrating but also a limiter. As my training progressed I found that as my legs fatigued, I would load one leg with more strain, which would in turn stress the other knee. My pain would bounce from one leg to the other. Understanding the root of the problem was essential to fixing it. Most of my problems stemmed from weak glutes. Strength training was essential to help these muscles, along with developing stronger adductors and abductors. These built-up muscles, along with keeping my iliotibial (IT) band (the muscle between your knee and hip) as relaxed as possible, would eventually help take the stress off the kneecaps. This process was frustrating and long, but necessary. If I wanted to run comfortably I had to play by the rules and add the required strength training. After months of training, my hard work paid off. My knees no longer hurt. This was a lesson I wish I had learned much earlier. If you heed the advice of physical therapy to increase your strength, you do have the ability to overcome certain injuries.

Having lots of time to think and rationalize around the impending goal, I realized this was purely a personal challenge. I compete against no one except myself. The voice that strikes during a run that questions my physical stability and tests my mental preparedness was one I could only answer myself. This was going to be my game. The question I often challenged myself with was, *is my body prepared well enough?* This question could only be answered during race day.

Nutrition is also a key element when planning for a 140.6 race. I realized early on that if I fueled my body properly, my endurance training would be much more efficient. I calculated my dietary needs that would allow for sustained training. I also incorporated the nutrition gels on training day in order to get my body prepared for the race. I factored in drinking sports drinks, salt, gels, and water. The race day diet seemed odd, but I went with what the experts had established. This was a plan that was set on the recommended carbs, protein, and fat based on my current height and weight. This part of the training plan was critical. I had heard too much about the official "bonk," otherwise known as hitting the wall. This is when the body gets low on glycogen stores which triggers fatigue. When running a marathon race after the swim and bike, your body ends up burning more fat and fewer carbs, making your body essentially inefficient. Therefore, I factored in the potential heat the course was going to offer by looking at the weather trends from prior years in The Woodlands, Texas. I also read that you should never try anything new on the course if you haven't tested it out at home in order to avoid GI issues. The day was going to be demanding enough. Who needs any additional hurdles to cross?

Closing in on race day, my physical therapist and I decided that KT Tape would be a great option during the race to keep my patella tracking better. I had also experienced the Graston technique, which is where a spatula-like tool is used repetitively to help bring blood flow to the top layer of your skin. I had had my thighs down to my knees massaged with this technique and had since accumulated a bruise that took up about 50 percent of my thighs. Between the rash from the KT Tape and the bruising from the massage, I could personally demonstrate my commitment to the sport—while offering friends and family plenty of reasons to laugh and question my sanity.

It was now five days before the start of the race. I was on a quest to succeed and accomplish an extreme fitness challenge. I share my personal thoughts here as a human trying to push my own limits while being in the middle of something both terrifying and exciting. I was ready to embrace a challenge and what may seem unachievable, but I would not let it hold me back. Capturing my thoughts and opinions is sometimes tough to do. I had silly dreams over the last few days before the race, which seemed to describe my insecurities regarding what was to come. I am a proud person, but I also function as someone with legitimate fears of the unknown. One of my dreams involved flying to the race. I was sitting next to a passenger who was twirling a ring on his finger. I noted it had the M-Dot (Ironman logo) on it and was super excited to engage with a former triathlete. He told me he had conquered Texas last year, and to my excitement asked to share his experience. He thoroughly described the swim as two to three feet tall waves with a wind speed of 45 mph that constantly pushed against your face. He pointed to behind his kneecap and said, “If this muscle isn’t built up, you won’t move an inch.” I then grabbed the back of my leg and thought to myself, I have never once worked that muscle behind my kneecap. This was a moment when I wasn’t sure if I had done enough. I woke up concerned that I had inadequacies or flaws in my plan of attack. I questioned if I were capable and competent enough. I then came to the realization that I had truly given it my all. I had followed the plan, I had tracked my nutrition, and I had incorporated rest. I was simply at the mercy of the day. I could go in confidently knowing that whatever the outcome, I had done my job. I had completed the daily workouts that slowly built up over time. The training plan had come to an end.

Three days out, I woke up realizing that my flight to Texas was the next day. My bags were packed, my bike had been shipped. I had sent out an email to share the event itinerary with my family. I had also talked about what a journey and challenge of life-balance this had become. I teared up on the way to work that morning because I heard a song regarding a journey. While I wasn't sure of the song meaning, the word journey resonated very deeply with me. I also had funny thoughts cross my mind. I thought about the time my daughter asked what I think about during my long runs. Before I could answer, she made clicking sounds. I asked her what she was doing and she said, "Mom, rest assured. Those clicking sounds are just the arthritis building up in your kneecaps."

My children have always been my strength. They were my rite of passage to become a role model and provider. One afternoon, I was talking to my daughter and she said, "Mom, I was talking about you at school today." She told me that she always talks about me and went on to remind me of how proud of me she is. She continued to remind me of how hard I have worked. That was when I realized that this journey wasn't just about me any longer. I had made it an opportunity to explore feelings with my children. I had set up a legacy which I hope my children will never forget. No matter the outcome of the upcoming race, my most important accomplishment was to teach my children to never give up, that a dream can be a reality, and that with hard work, dedication, and devotion you can accomplish anything. You don't have to be the best, but you do have to aspire to be the best you. I was humbled by what I had learned about myself. I had sought after something deeper and more spiritual through this experience. This was my way of proving to myself that I can—and I will—overcome any hurdles presented to me.

I looked over at the calendar on my cubicle wall at work. It was May 13, 2015. My Ironman training-plan journey had started on December 1 and the calendar had each of my daily workouts identified and written out. A big "X" marked with a sharpie signified the completion of a workout commitment. An accomplishment and achievement with each daily square marked off. The pages of detailed, completed workouts throughout the months reminded me of the voyage I had chosen to partake in. I looked at it then with three unchecked days and could feel the validity of my desire to conquer this challenge. I wrote down these thoughts with simple tears in my eyes, knowing that in three days this would be the start of a memory. I wanted to document these feelings before the race because I thought it important to capture the spirit in the moment. I had dedicated so much of my time to balance life in general. The past six months had been trying, exhausting, rewarding, and demanding. They had allowed me to dig deeper than I ever had in order to be race ready. Training for an Ironman has had both its highs and lows. It has created feelings of doubt and inadequacy, while also boosting my confidence and eagerness to display my commitment to the sport. The excitement, challenge, and unknown outcomes of the event made me feel uneasy, but I was also contemplating the completion, the flight home, and the emptiness I would for sure experience after the race. I tried to push those thoughts aside and envelop myself in the excitement, but that feeling echoed deep with what may be next to come.

It was an exciting day. I had depleted my glycogen store over the last few days and kept my carbs to 35 percent for three days. It had been difficult. Who knew how easy it is to accumulate carbs? Picking a healthy diet that excluded them was quite difficult. Finally, I would get to carb-load with a 75 percent carb diet, which excited me. It's like I was in candy land and could indulge in the foods I enjoy. There was a pizza party at work and for the first time I would get to partake in the festivities. In the past, I was always in the salad line, even going as far as excluding tempting desserts. But this day I would participate. An hour before lunch I apologized to my coworkers for my impending behavior; I planned to eat like a fourteen-year-old boy. I could even say I have the ability to eat like my eleven-year-old son. One day of football practice and a growth spurt can clear out the refrigerator. My son can devour a large pizza in one sitting while still having the figure of a green bean. I can consume a pizza but my lean figure could easily morph into a pear shape. But all this hard work allowed me to throw caution to the wind—pear or not, I would partake and enjoy my reward.

During the evening I would meet with my physical therapist one last time. She had been superb in ensuring I follow the plan for healthy knees and legs. After that I planned to enjoy a night with my family. I wanted to leave the talk of the race behind and have it just be about the family. There would be plenty of time for discussing the race. Over the last six months I had consumed my family and friends with my highs and lows, and I was sure they were excited about closure. I bet they questioned my thought process on "what's next" but I would address that question when it needed to be addressed.

Game On

The alarm went off at 3 a.m. Wake up! It was time to fly to Texas. I gathered my luggage which was loaded with everything and anything I could find that was identified on my packing checklist. This list was three times the size of my original sprint triathlon list. This day required my own nutrition, watches, power meters, compression clothing—just to name a few items. My bike (now a road bike modified to include aerobars, which I named "Pearl") was shipped to the race the week prior, hoping that this would ease the stress of travel. We loaded the car and off we went to the airport.

While sitting at Logan Airport, we came upon another couple that was headed to Texas. They were proudly sporting their race gear, so we gingerly headed over to make conversation and acquire last-minute tips and tricks. The nice couple were elite competitors, so I knew my conversation would be on an amateur level while theirs was with clear, defined goals in mind. As lots of athletes are built to compete at their maximum capacity, sometimes they seem to forget that it can be very nerve-racking to those who are there to push their limits and focus on completing the race within the seventeen hours. So comparing training plans can be a downer and allow you to question your preparedness. I tried to repeat the mantra that I followed the plan to the end, and now it will be up to all of the elements to decide my fate. Heat, humidity, UV, nutrition, mental, and physical game would be the deciding factors. Not talking to other couples that have different goals in mind.

When discussing goals, it is easy to feel overwhelmed or even insecure or inadequate. These thoughts are normal, but it is important to remember that each athlete has their own personal goal. Mine was set to complete the course in the given seventeen hours. As mentioned earlier, we all have different lifestyles, our training is unique, and our talents vary. I was a swimmer in high school and running was not in my field of view, while other athletes were maybe cross-country fanatics. It's important to reflect on your own personal journey and not everyone else's. As the years have passed, I have met a variety of athletes: those recovering from addiction, injury, medical conditions, and many other obstacles. My race is for me. I will not let my insecurities and/or inadequacies consume my thoughts. I have done the work to the best of my ability and am worthy of the competition.

I had trained in snow, snow, and more snow. Landing in Texas and feeling the heat penetrate my face was an awakening. This was going to be a challenge. We gathered my belongings, rented a car, and headed to the Ironman pre-registration desk. Now we were two days out from the big race. The anticipation was at my fingertips. After registering, I made my way to the merchandise store to purchase gear to sport my accomplishment: stickers for the car, mugs, sweatshirts, key chains—you name it. I was in the moment, excited about the events to come. All was good; body in check, my mood was excellent, and life was extremely exciting.

The day before the race I had an opportunity to check out the lake for the first time. The swim portion was a fear of mine, since I didn't have the opportunity to get any lake swims in prior to the race. Of course, everything you read highly suggests that you get lake swims in prior to any official race. So my mind remained uneasy, my thoughts telling me that I may be unprepared for what's to come. Pool workouts were far different from lake swimming. There are no lane guides in a lake. We were given an hour to swim the lake and become comfortable with water visibility, sighting, and temperature. Therefore, thousands of athletes showed up to become comfortable with the race conditions. Rolling into the water behind all the other athletes, the reality of the event was hitting home. Tomorrow at this time I would be at the mercy of the course and I hoped that all events would go without a hitch. Still concerned about the wetsuit event of the 70.3 race—and remembering the moment where I thought breathing through a straw would be much simpler—I decided that no matter what the water temperature would be, I would go in my tri suit, otherwise referred to as a tri kit. My toes touched the water and I was oh so pleasantly surprised at the eighty-degree temperature. *I can do this. This is my time.* These were the thoughts that pranced around my head. I swam a short course as a few of the swim markers allowed you to get a good feeling of direction and sighting. That is how an athlete does their best to stay on course. Keeping mile markers in sight in order to not add additional yards to the swim is important. Every minute counts. I swam at ease with fellow athletes from all over the world. It was a fun way to meet people and hear about their journey. This was a melting pot of athletes who all decided to accept this challenge as well. It was truly a kumbaya moment. Upon returning to shore, we received our mandatory briefings that concentrated on the Texas heat and staying hydrated throughout the day, as well as course considerations. It was important to know if there were areas of concern on the bike ride like sharp turns off a steep hill. These briefings are designed to keep athletes safe and aware. They also addressed racing rules and allowed folks to raise questions or concerns.

A few days prior to the race I had thought this would be a great opportunity to explore Texas and make a mini vacation out of it. To my discovery, I was wrong. The two days leading up to the race left very little time for anything else. So, for future note: If I were to consider another opportunity and wanted to build in some R & R time, I suggest adding a few extra days as a buffer prior to the two race-prep days.

Next day was race day, when the rubber meets the pavement, and when the unknowns and the insecurities start to bubble up. It's important to embrace the spirit and rely on your hard work, and try to place all of the anxiety on the back burner. Oh, what a beautiful night it was! I had dinner consisting mostly of carbs. Spirits were high and, surprisingly, I was feeling tired yet anxious. 3 a.m. was approaching quickly and so by 9:30 p.m. we were nestled in bed for a time to decompress and get some well-required sleep. That was until about 11 p.m. when the neighbors thought it would be appropriate to move the party to their room. That was it, my hour and a half of sleep would have to carry me the remainder of the night and throughout the entire day and evening. My mind raced about what was to come, what would my expected results be, and did I pack enough nutrition? By 2 a.m. I was up and happily doing the Warrior I yoga pose in my room.

Breakfast was a predefined meal since I knew what worked for me. I didn't want to try anything different the morning of the race. I was on the other side of the country and the thought of eating from a restaurant menu could prove detrimental to my race. Therefore, I stuck with cereal, yogurt, banana, and a bagel which were tightly stored in a small refrigerator in the hotel room. At 3 a.m. I tried my best to eat my breakfast but this proved very difficult following a huge carb dinner the night before. Eating all of those carbs was challenging and didn't feel very pleasing. I didn't want anything. I was a blimp at maximum capacity trying to suck down more carbs. Yikes, to think of all those yummy, fruity, gummy snacks that I would have for seventeen long hours seemed less than desirable at this point. I knew my breakfast was an important and very essential part of fueling for the event ahead and so I slowly consumed my previously prepared meal.

At 4:45 a.m. we left the hotel in the pitch darkness, with an eerie feeling. The roads were quiet on the drive in and butterflies were stirring in my stomach as adrenaline was building. When we arrived at the race we needed to drop off the transition bags. This included two additional transition bags for special needs along the way. Special needs transition bags are used to store items that may be needed along the course, like body glide, an extra pair of socks, or additional nutrition items. Any items placed in special needs would not be returned to athletes post-race.

Part of the morning routine was to check on your bike one last time prior to the start. We were warned during the athlete briefing to have our bike tires stay slightly below our normal air levels, to adjust for the rising temperature throughout the day. At this time, all athletes were feeling their nerves kick in. The ominous sound of random tires bursting on the bike racks in the background was very intimidating. I was feeling the stress, hoping that when I came out of the water, my bike would still have two wheels ready to go. Race-day weather was predicted to reach 89 degrees, with 90 percent humidity, and an extreme UV level. They were also calling for a 20 percent chance of rain and thunderstorms in the afternoon. Race-day temperatures ended up topping out at 97 degrees with a 100 percent humidity level, proving a very rough, challenging race day.

I was off to body markings with the volunteers. People get excited about drawing on you with thick black markers. The one thing I can offer about that morning is that the voluntary staff was amazing. They were everywhere and were willing and committed to assist us with everything and anything in their power. They packed a smile that left you feeling confident and enthusiastic about what was to come.

It was then time to line up in the swim corral. I had estimated that the swim would take me approximately one hour and forty minutes. I made this assumption based on it not being a chlorine pool; there would have to be some maneuvering around fellow competitors; I would have to sight more; and I wanted to pace myself to leave plenty of reserve energy for the bike and run. It was going to be a very long day.

The race had a rolling start based on time. They had people holding signs with times in ten-minute increments. The pros and the physically challenged get a head start. After that the fifty-minute swimmers are raring to go, and I was jealous and in awe of the folks who can swim at such a fast speed for 2.4 miles. Speaking with fellow athletes in the swim start line, I learned that you should place yourself within ten minutes from your actual swim pace. Therefore, I seated myself at the one-and-a-half-hour range. I was surrounded by approximately 3,000 athletes at this time. Between the athletes and the cheering squads, the excitement and adrenaline hit an all-time high.

I couldn't tell if a gun had gone off but judging by the commotion and adrenaline, the race had begun. We started to walk and edge closer and closer towards the dock and within ten minutes I was jumping off the dock into the water. It was 6:40 a.m. and the sun was starting to peek through the clouds. The water was chilly and my immediate thought was to quickly separate myself as fast as possible from the rest of the athletes. This part of the race is called the washing machine, as it is chaotic swimming with 3,000 of your closest friends. Arms were flailing and legs were kicking. I quickly made my place in the water and set sail. The journey that I had prepared myself for during the last six months was in motion. My thoughts were pure and uneventful. I considered looking at my watch to see if my pace was on par with my training, but I decided that this would not change my effort. Rather than getting discouraged I kept encouraging myself to stay focused, maintain good swim form, and control my breathing. It was important to constantly remind myself to sight as well to ensure I was staying on course. It was easy to determine when I was approaching thc halfway point since this was identified by the color of the buoys. The buoys remained orange until the turn-around point was indicated by a red buoy. At this point I still opted out of looking at my watch, deciding not to allow my time to dictate my pace.

Unfortunately, like lots of triathletes fighting for real estate or maybe just due to the ignorance of your surroundings, I did take a kick to the face and claws to the legs randomly. Some athletes have had their goggles ripped right off. Not a fun way to finish out the race without them. This is not a fun experience. It's tough since you are mostly looking into the water while swimming and you're breathing off to the side. It means you are less familiar with your surroundings until you lift your head to sight. If you are pacing faster or slower than someone else, you are likely to collide. Therefore, when you seat yourself during the pre-start of the swim, I suggest that you start with your predicted time pace. This will help lessen the likelihood of colliding with someone else. As I was not going for any world records, I elected to stay towards the outside. I ventured away from the buoys and distanced myself from the other racers as much as possible.

I was en route just before the turn-around buoy, when the unthinkable happened: my left calf cramped. I had experienced this in the pool before, but laps are a short distance and it's easy to find time to stretch out and recompose. Within minutes my right calf also started to cramp. The feeling was very painful, almost like a charley horse. You know that uneasy, daggering feeling that you don't want to touch your leg, but you also feel like you should massage it to help relieve the discomfort? I gathered strength to not quit at this point in the race. It was way too soon and I have overcome challenges in the past. I decided to swim with my arms only. I flipped onto my back temporarily but quickly learned that it was also painful. I stopped, trying to massage the daggers of spasms my legs felt, but that was unachievable. As I tried to massage my legs, I would start to sink and with so many other swimmers in the area it wasn't safe to stay in one spot. After a few minutes of swimming with my arms only, the pain started to lessen in my calves. I was hoping that this was a one-time ordeal. Another swimmer approached me, and upon his impending stroke he hit my calves. They seized up again. I had to shut off the pain and pray that after the swim completion I would be able to walk and continue on.

I entered an area of the swim race close to the finish, and the water was choppy as the channel got narrower. I focused my energy on the cheering crowd that greeted everyone towards the exit of the swim. Hands reached out and grabbed my two arms to help assist me up the stairs. Wow, I could walk! How could this be? I had assumed I would be headed to the medic tent with charley horses consuming me for the remainder of the day.

That's when I picked out that unique cowbell in the distance, looked up, and heard my name being shouted. I started to gain strength with each step as I edged closer to my husband. Smiling from ear to ear, I knew my husband was so proud of what I had accomplished. With self-affirmation I reminded myself that the first hurdle of the day was behind me. I glanced at my watch. Wow! One hour and thirty-four minutes—a personal record for me. This was amazing considering I primarily used my arms and shoulders to swim. I wondered how much better my time may have been if I could have engaged my legs. My triathlon books had mentioned that during the swim, the important part was keeping your legs up. As your legs drop deeper into the water, the more drag you create which slows you down. So maybe my ability to stay horizontal with forward momentum helped to make sure that the cramps weren't too detrimental to my swim. I was already critiquing my performance but it did not diminish my excitement for a swim that went beyond my expectations.

Running towards the bike transition was interesting. As the helpers assisted in transition, you could hear tires still popping in the background as predicted. As the day heated up, so did the tires, and while resting on the transition rack, the tires would succumb to the heat and explode. Some athletes were barely out of the water and couldn't get a fair shake. I guess this is why everyone has their own story to tell. I felt badly for the competitors who were in need of assistance and didn't even know it yet. I also feared what lay ahead on this course and hoped my bike would fare well with the rising temperature along the course. It was going to be a very long day.

In and out of T1, I was headed for 112 miles of heat, humidity, and nothing to entertain myself with but my own thoughts. I was curious what this leg of the race would bring. Having approximately eight hours alone was going to be a challenge. I knew that during the run there would intermittently be some adult communication but this was a new place for me. So I told myself to enjoy the scenery and appreciate what Texas has to offer. I tried singing songs to myself to keep my mind occupied from bringing on negative thoughts, but oddly enough it was very difficult to remember the lyrics. Maybe the heat was getting to me, but when singing Katy Perry's song, I could only belt out "Hear me rooaaarr." That was it. The rest was a blank. I was at a loss for words. Maybe I was getting delusional, but good old Christmas carols were the only songs I could come up with. I had just left snow, was excited about sun and heat, and then went right back to "let it snow, let it snow, let it snow." This was comically concerning as I felt mentally I had hit a new, slightly entertaining, low.

I found myself using markers to help progress. At mile twenty-five, I was nearly a quarter done with eighty-seven to go. Likewise, when I was fifty miles in, I was nearing the halfway point. At one time during the ride, my self-esteem was boosted as I heard the course official on his motorcycle ride up next to me. There were strict rules enforced by Ironman and the no-drafting rule was one of the strictest. All riders must stay twelve meters (almost forty feet) behind another rider. If a rider chooses to pass it must be done within twenty-five seconds. They warned the man next to me to pass within three more seconds, which he didn't, and he was penalized five minutes. Wow, someone had drafted off me. Mrs. Slow-go Conservative was being drafted. It actually felt good, although I laughed thinking I was a unique choice since my pace was concerning at best. A definite ego boost.

Throughout the race I would hear athletes remind me that my race bib top was sliding up my back. Not thinking a whole lot about it, I tugged the material down towards my shorts, but in due time it would rise up again and I would forget all about it. Well, after spending most of the day in an aerodynamic position under the Texas sun, my skin would pay a heavy price. Still to this day, I have a discoloration reminder on my lower back—nearly five years later.

As the day went on, the heat must have taken its toll on bikers, because there were tire tubes littered throughout the course with dozens of racers tending to their damaged bikes. I tried to block out any negative thoughts of this occurring to me. My one and only quest at this point was to hit the course cut-off times with enough of a buffer to complete the run.

The enormous 112-mile loop wasn't all that bad. There were times of baking in the sun, along with some areas of shade that gave you moments to enjoy a light, cooler breeze. The course was considered flat compared to other Ironman venues. It was very hot and there were times when the wind was in my face. The bike ride would prove doable as long as I nailed my nutrition, remained hydrated, and consumed enough salt to offset any loss through perspiration. Rounding completion, the reckless sound of cowbells, air horns, and crowds of people cheering us on was amazing. Strangers cared. They wanted me and every other athlete on that course to succeed. The atmosphere was electric, and the energy kept us all moving forward. I homed in on that unique cowbell sound and found my eager husband waving at me. I blew him a kiss and strutted off. I headed towards the tents to gear up for the run. Two legs of the race done, with one monster 26.2-mile run away from completing this badass race.

This was it. I was heading out of the third and final T2 tent. I was approximately ten hours in with a seven-hour run buffer to complete this journey. My legs felt decent, not super strong but tough enough to withstand the third and final obstacle. It felt like I was an arm's length from earning the Ironman title. I started off with the run-walk-run method. Here we go, another newbie mistake. I had used my Garmin race watch from the start of the swim, throughout the bike ride, and then on to the run. By mile two into the run, my GPS watch was beating low battery, and soon officially dead. This was a deflating and mentally brutal hurdle I needed to overcome. I had no accurate way of pacing my RWR-method. *Shake it off, suck it up, and continue forward one step at a time*, I told myself over and over again.

OK, my thoughts were positive and I was feeling confident until I hit the dreaded three-mile marker. This is the point people refer to when they talk about "hitting the wall." Boy, not only did I hit it, but I wanted to jump over it and end this race. Thoughts crossed my mind like, *Can I really make it another twenty-three miles?* and "*Am I strong enough?*" The negative thought started to affect me. I read that it is important to kick these thoughts and replace them with positive affirmations, or mantras, immediately. I needed to take this one mile at a time, which is way more achievable in my mind. I was a kick-ass athlete and would get through this journey.

Hours went by, and thinking had become difficult. Trying to figure out the math without my watch was nearly impossible. The running course was three laps and asking people what mile we were on was hard since other runners were on different laps than me. So I was independent on my journey to complete this. Eating gels, bananas, and carb discs while drinking Gatorade, water, and Red Bulls was getting more and more difficult as the race progressed. It's important to understand that the body can't function well in these types of environments and distances—with the heat, humidity, and UV index as high as they were—without maintaining proper nutrition. I reminded myself that I couldn't stop keeping my body nourished and hydrated—no matter what—if I wanted to complete this.

As always, every race is a learning experience and, trying to be a well-prepared athlete, I had taken preventative measures. I read in books that gulping too much air during the swim could cause GI issues. I was also concerned that the relentless heat throughout the day could cause headaches. Therefore, I tried to plan by having some preventive medicine at hand. My running belt consisted of a big pocket in the front. I thought to make my life easier, I would place both Advil and Tums directly into the bag for ease of access. I then placed my gels and jelly beans directly into the bag as well. Without much consideration throughout the race, I poured water down my neck and back along with loading my tri gear with ice cubes to remain cool. What I failed to realize was that the Tums and

Advil would disintegrate all over my snacks, creating a rainbow effect down my black tri shorts. I had a beautiful array of pastel colors that even Bob Ross would have admired.

For us evening runners the course offered chicken broth and for once I felt like I was feasting at a five-star restaurant. It was a welcoming and soothing comfort food. The course also offered pickle juice, which was unheard of to me, but athletes seemed to gravitate towards it. During another training day for a future event, I will probably investigate how it feels to consume this, but definitely not today. My stomach was already starting to rumble from all of the carbs.

The course offered lots of entertainment to help take your mind off the incredible drain. There were people dancing and singing, playing drums, and a variety of signs to make us laugh. There were also parts of the course where the entertainment value dropped, and you were left to your own devices of self-thought and reflection. Those were the parts where I started to become more mentally self-destructive.

It was difficult to pass the medic tents and hear fellow comrades moaning in pain from various cramps, wounds, dehydration, or nausea and not feel the immensity of the challenge still before me. The pre-race brief officials did their best to prepare race participants for the conditions and highlighted the need to hydrate in order to prevent dehydration. I met fellow runners along the course that said they went to the medic tents and passed out or took a nap for a half hour to overcome the ill effects of the heat, humidity, and high UV index before continuing on.

By lap two, nightfall was setting in. There were dark moments on the course, and it seemed all too easy to quit and give into the temptation of finding a voluntary staff member, plead my case of physical and mental discomforts, and take the ATV back to the safety net of my husband. These thoughts that resided in the back of my mind took the race to a level I had never experienced before. For the first time ever, I felt vulnerable and defeated. Exhaustion and food deprivation were grabbing hold. At such a low, I was completing my second lap and rounding the corner when I spotted my eager husband cheering me on. His smile gleamed with pride and encouragement. The significance of the race resonated deeply in my moment of despair. He reminded me of how far I'd come and told me I couldn't give up now. I didn't work this hard to quit at the final stage of this race. I quickly shared my thoughts of self-doubt. He then retorted with his thoughts of gratification and accomplishment that I will triumph. My ego was put to the test, and at that moment I just decided to carry on. I would not stop. If my legs were willing to continue on, then I wouldn't be the one to stop them.

Lap three was by far the most difficult challenge. A dark course and a thinned-out race. Parts of the run went through the windy, dark trails of Lake Woodlands. Glow sticks were handed out to alert people in the area. Some people had been smart enough to pack headlamps to help navigate through the darker parts of the course. Midnight was closing in quickly. I would ask other racers if completion by midnight was even possible at this point of the race and everyone was always very optimistic. The thought of a DNF (Did Not Finish) was a blemish on my ego that I would not accept willingly. I would spend a few minutes with a racer and in time they would either head out quicker or drift off. It was a race where you embraced the comfort of talking to someone and sharing bits and pieces regarding your drive for completion. It was always a recurring theme that running to set a great example for your children ranked the most important. We would set short course goals like sprinting every other cone and then walking. I learned that having a meaning and a purpose was an essential skill to keep a forward momentum.

Meeting up with my husband on the third and final lap inspired me. I knew this rite of passage was nearing completion. With some encouraging words and positive reinforcement, I was approaching the end. My husband decided it was time to give some tough love and told me to pull up my big-girl panties and finish what I had chosen to start. I felt like I needed a stern lecture to keep my head in the game. To this day we still joke about that. My pace needed to be picked up, and I would need to dig deeper than ever before if I wanted to assume the title of completion within the given time constraint. He headed over to the finish line while I trotted the remainder of the course. I could hear ranting and raving and the announcer proudly calling competitors out by their names, stating that they were an Ironman. It was so surreal. My husband said, "You hear that? You did it! I am heading over to the finishing shoot and I will see you there." I grinned knowing this journey was nearly complete. As he veered to the left towards the red carpet, my course navigated to the right. I was confused, and the announcer's voice started to dissipate. It was getting fainter and fainter with each step. That's when I noticed the mile marker. I was at mile twenty-four. I still had 2.2 miles to go. Tears streamed down my face. The taste of victory was at my fingertips, and yet the course had more punishment to dole out. I felt misled and my thoughts again turned negative. I could hear each footstep painfully hit the pavement again. I was alone. However, my inclination was that I could not stop, I had to fight against the pain and push through.

It was nearly twenty-five minutes later when the sounds of thousands of people got closer and closer. The crowd applauded and I could hear people screaming my name along with the other athletes that were still in my field of view. The crowds of people beat down on the sidewalls of the finish line. I could feel the beautiful, red, plushy carpet under my tired, achy feet. At that moment in time, I felt no pain throughout my body for the remaining run to the finish line. My breath became shallow and for the first time ever in my life the feeling was beyond overwhelming. It was all so surreal. Hundreds of people leaned over seeking high fives. It made the past six months coalesce into a moment of triumph and victory. Tears streamed down my face. Seeing my husband, I appreciated everything I had worked for. What I had experienced through my journey would be something I could explain in detail to others, but only those who had accepted the same challenge could ever understand what it all meant.

The medal was placed around my neck while medics asked if I needed assistance. I was whisked away for a photo op. Finally, I was ushered over to see my husband. We hugged and kissed and took it all in. I proceeded to the massage tent where I realized just how tight my calves were. I begged the lady to go very gentle in order to not stir up another charley horse. Then on to the food—yes, pizza, of all things. I thought that with all the carbs throughout the day I would be unable to tolerate pizza but it was amazing. Of course, I had read that I could burn anywhere between 10–13,000 calories that day, almost a week's allowance of food. Guilt-free I devoured the pizza. It was one of the most amazing-tasting dinners I have ever feasted on.

That Hurt

The trip back to the hotel was a half-hour drive. I craved a nice, hot shower to ease my muscles and clean off the lake water, sunblock, and sweat. I took off my sneakers and to my dismay both my socks and sneakers were covered in blood. Another rookie mistake. I should have used Vaseline or body glide prior to placing my timing chip on my ankle. The friction from the sneaker and the rub of the chip had torn straight through my skin. It created a wound worthy of a doctor's visit upon returning home. As I stepped into the shower I screamed like a twelve-year-old girl at a haunted house. I wasn't quite sure of where the pain I was enduring came from, until I saw my legs. The abrasiveness of my bike seat and my tri shorts had done a job on my legs. The burn looked like I had sat down on a seat of fire. Why didn't I remember reading anything on this? Where was the information to prepare me for what to expect post-race? If only I had taken the necessary precautions. I take this opportunity to share my experience to hopefully help other new athletes to prepare for the unexpected. I sat in the tub at 2 a.m. sobbing. Once again, this was a journey towards learning and accepting the idea that we aren't invincible.

This was more than a physical achievement. It was a mental accomplishment, too. My wounds were skin-deep but my ego was exposed to a new sort of self-learning. That night, I didn't relish in my accomplishment. I felt sad and couldn't grasp why I was feeling that way. My goal was complete. I had trained to finish this race. I worked hard, nourished my body, did everything according to plan, and met the mission. So what was my problem?

All of my superficial wounds healed with time and were just gentle reminders of everything I had endured throughout the race. Nothing could have prepared me for the lessons I was going to learn throughout this day both mentally and physically. Therefore, that was the most important reason to write this journal; I never wanted to forget all of the details of what went into accomplishing this challenging feat.

I slept fairly decently that night, which was nice as it had been nearly two days since I had a good night's rest. The next morning we headed to the breakfast buffet, with me walking like Frankenstein's monster and wishing I had one of those blow-up donut seats in hand. We met some other athletes and made small talk. Although not fully relishing the accomplishment yet, my husband shared photos and told me how proud he was of me. When I checked my phone, I had tons of texts from our children, family, and friends cheering me on. My husband showed me how he had shared a play-by-play with them as the day unfolded. This brought the day's first smile to my face.

At the airport, waiting to fly home, it was easy to pick out fellow racers with our signature walks or shirts that displayed our victories. We met a young couple that had also completed the event and we shared our experiences with one another. "What's next?" they wanted to know. They guaranteed that I would be back for another race. They enthusiastically shared that they had already signed up for three other events planned throughout the year. I reiterated that I was forty and could check this one off my bucket list. I had always enjoyed an opportunity to do some crazy stuff over the years, including diving with sharks, skydiving, bungee jumping, etc. But this challenge was not only physically taxing—the mental game far exceeded my expectations. I swore to myself I would never do this again. My goals were met and I could move on with new adventures, or so I thought.

On the way home, I reflected on what I had accomplished. Revisiting the darker thoughts and discussing them with my family helped me understand that I am human. My deepest, darkest, and happiest moments during the race were normal. I hit every emotion possible in the seventeen-hour period. I wasn't prepared for the emotional struggle throughout race day. Watching post-race footage of fellow racers sharing their experience made me understand that I was not alone in my view of the race unfolding.

Days later I began to embrace the experience. I embarked on the mission of revisiting all the events that took place to get me to the starting line. The deep devotion to living room workouts, the cold runs in the middle of winter, the aches and pains of muscle fatigue, and the countless hours of tracking foods and modifying schedules to accommodate family, work, and business trips. This also included the coordination of working around daily schedules to include family commitments, never wanting to lose sight of giving my children and family attention. It added up to an indescribable determination to never give up and to keep up with the schedule. All of these details were essential to finding balance in order to accomplish this Ironman journey.

After completing the race, I presented our previously purchased souvenirs to my children. The shirt I purchased for my daughter said "Future Ironman," which I thought was cute. What I didn't see coming was my daughter sticking duct tape on the back of her shirt with the writing "My mom completed an Ironman," and then wearing it to school. She came home saying how proud she was and how she had bragging rights to her friends. This was my first authentic smile throughout completion of the race. My message had come across loud and clear to my children. Perseverance and determination, along with strong willpower, can carry you through anything. Having my family's love, support, and commitment from day one was the strength I used to carry me to the end. As I stated in the very beginning of my writings, I wrote this as a piece for my children to read, hoping to see how this may inspire them someday. I want them to embrace a challenge; how what may seem unachievable will actually motivate and stimulate the need to fulfill their dream. I don't push or encourage them to follow my path, but I hope that I teach and inspire them to see what is possible through action. If something seems unachievable, step back, reevaluate, and develop a strategy to help initiate and conquer. This will hopefully create even more opportunities, but most importantly create self-awareness, self-esteem, and a belief that all is possible.

Two weeks after earning the Ironman title I was excited to share details of my race with anyone who wanted to discuss it. Of course, the people in my life had for six months heard every detail of my preparation work—along with all the details of training, my restricted diet, and my ailments suffered along the way. My husband and I were sitting on the couch reviewing my times against fellow competitors in my age group. This lead to conversations regarding the weather conditions and the heat and if I could've picked up my speed. I tried to keep reserve energy in the tank during the ride to ensure I would have enough for the run. If I would run a cooler race, I could probably exert less energy and, therefore, shave time off my ride. Also, if I could safeguard my calves and take preventive measures, then I could hopefully avoid charley horses during the swim. My transition times seemed like I had acted leisurely, like I may have stopped to have a picnic in-between. As discussions ensued, anticipation got the best of me. I remember chanting to myself during the race that I would never do this again. But there is something about a triathlete that only another triathlete gets and that is the drive towards self-improvement. I get that I will never be elite. Heck, I will probably remain close to the end of the pack. Still, I have ambition, which can be both good and bad.

I reserve the right to always challenge myself and to never stop believing in my body and mind. I need goals, a reason to live, and to try my hardest. Give me any challenge that I deem important to me and I will persevere. I couldn't resist the challenge of racing another Ironman with the opportunity to cut a minute, or maybe even hour, off my time and achieve a new personal record. So I went shopping for another 140.6 race. I discovered lots of new races, but of course I was on a list of thousands of people who book these events years in advance. It would be a challenge to find a new race this late in the year. But as fate would have it, I secured another 140.6 race: Ironman in Tempe, Arizona. It was scheduled for November 15, 2015—six months out. This would allow me another couple of months of recovery before resuming the schedules, the workouts, watching my nutrition, and discussing all of my highs and lows with family and friends. I was so excited to start a new journey.

Redemption

So, what would I do differently regarding training now that I had the ability to train throughout the summer in Massachusetts? For starters, the long rides and runs in the home along with ice baths in the snow were behind me. The opportunity to train in temperatures that would be closer to the actual race temperatures should prove helpful. The Arizona course was rated easier than Texas so hopefully it wouldn't be too difficult to reach a new PR. I considered seeking the opportunity to ride with a bike group in order to stay motivated and push my limits. I also wanted to train using a heart rate monitor faithfully. I did use one on the runs, but I didn't make it a practice to train more efficiently. I have also learned that whenever an injury arises, it's better to back off and address it immediately.

My training would also incorporate a good swim plan. My training for Texas consisted of swimming in circles for hours at the local pool, which is only fifty meters long. I did not incorporate speed training. I followed my training plan leisurely. With all of that being said, I will always respect my body to the highest degree. I realize that as I age, I need to remember that feeling thirty is not actually the same thing as being thirty. I seek goals and opportunities but will always admire what our bodies are capable of. I am in awe that a human body does have the ability to travel great distances. Anything is possible with discipline, focus, and drive. My goals had been met with Texas, but I aspired to improve. I was determined to do great things and to learn from my mistakes.

I love to share my story as I feel it's a great way to capture the events that got me to the starting line. I don't want my memory of events to fade away without the ability to take note of what got me there. It's important to journalize memories and thoughts to capture the highs and lows so that over time, as my memory degrades, my ability to recall what went into this monumental event will remain. I will stay humble to the fact that everyone is different and acts according to their abilities. I have learned that this journey isn't just about the mind and body learning to work in sync. It is about balance, support, fulfillment, commitment, and the willingness to put it all out there.

It was time for my second full-distance Ironman. Five and a half months out from race day, I decided to initiate some changes based on my last experience. My bike had two water bottle cages and I determined it would be more efficient to have an additional water bottle placed between my aerobars. This would help me stay in an aerodynamic position without having to lift my torso and create greater drag in order to stay hydrated. I also added a bike computer with RPM to measure cadence. My last computer just gave minutes per mile. If I were to improve my time, I needed to use RPM in conjunction with my heart rate. I've also found something called Hoo Ha glide cream. Interesting name. If it does what it says, I hoped to never endure another bike burn on a long ride again.

As suggested, my sneakers were replaced by two new pairs. I purchased a replacement wetsuit to use in lake swims. I needed to put mind over matter and overcome swimming with my coat of armor. Therefore, I came to the realization that I must purchase a new wetsuit in order to clear my mind of having another panic episode during the swim.

I mapped out my new plan. In order to become a stronger athlete, I initiated an intermediate plan with hopes of capturing a better PR. This time my focus would be on a combination of strength training along with my daily routines as identified in the plan. My knee doctor continued to tell me to add more cross-training to my regimen, and so I took his recommendation and applied myself to getting stronger.

Unlike training for Texas, I didn't need to train in harsh winter conditions. This time it wouldn't be as difficult acclimating to the heat. Also, when training for Texas I never had an opportunity to venture for a lake swim. In New England, the sprint and Olympic triathlons don't begin until late spring so this time would prove different. I would be more prepared. Four months out from race day I had already incorporated an Olympic and sprint triathlon. Any chance to run a 5K and I was there. My son also embraced many opportunities to run shorter-distance races with me. I called him my coach. He could run circles around me, but always kept me motivated and inspired me to improve. Sometimes he would remind me that I run like an old lady, but the banter and teasing was fun and always made our runs enjoyable. By mid-July, I was adapting to running during ninety-degree days. The 140.6-distance was more familiar to me. I could focus on trying to improve the end result rather than on whether I would be able to finish. That was not a question any longer. Although I had one 140.6 under my belt, I also couldn't become complacent with the unnerving task that I had committed to once again.

Arizona Ironman—commenced and completed. Success! My one major learning lesson from this event came again from the swim. My wetsuit felt great, but what I did not account for was the immense skin burn I wound endure from the collar of the suit and the rub on my neck. After a 2.4-mile swim, the friction between the two chafed a very deep skin burn. After the swim I made my way to the wetsuit strippers. What a treat. I lay down on my back and within ten seconds two men grabbed the shoulders of the suit and had it peeled off me like a naked banana. Upon exiting T1, I made my way to the sunscreen volunteers. A lady eagerly greeted me reminding me how important it was to cover my back with SPF in the Arizona heat. She graciously sprayed aerosol sunscreen all over my neck, arms, and legs. Within seconds I was in tears from the immense pain on my neck. *Shake it off.* I knew that within minutes the pain would subside, but I made note to read up and discover a solution to never ever let this happen again.

I had successfully taken an additional two hours off my race time compared to Texas earlier in the year. My hard work and ability to become more efficient had paid off. As mentioned previously, when you apply the lessons you have learned from prior races and become an even more informed athlete that is when improvements start to occur. I had grown as a person and realized that hard work and determination can make all the difference in the world. I took these new lessons and would continue to apply them towards future goals.

It's always fun to see forward progress over the years. During 2016 I could showcase my improvements and see where my hard work actually paid off. I signed up for the Vineman Ironman in Santa Rosa, California, which would take place on July 30. I also scheduled a repeat of Ironman Arizona for November 20. The Vineman was a beautiful venue with rolling hills through numerous vineyards. I couldn't wait for the race completion so that I could enjoy a lavish cheese board paired with some tasty cabernets. What a reward for all of my hard work.

The reward of course wouldn't be granted without some punishment. The swim and bike ride were challenging, but the views made it all worth it. After completing the bike ride, I headed over to T2. Placing my helmet and bike shoes in the transition bag, I then placed my race bib around my waist. I secured my Garmin watch on my wrist, lathered up in sunscreen, gulped a cup of water, and then trotted out to the third and final leg. The California heat was tough and as the afternoon hours approached, the temperature kept rising. Around thirteen miles into the run I glanced up towards the sun; the sky started spinning, black dots were consuming my field of view. I felt as though I might become sick. With fear of passing out, I found a nearby curb and sat down with my head between my knees. Athletes sprinting by were concerned. They would randomly stop and ask if everything was OK, and was there anything they could do? One very kind gentleman—till this day I wish I had asked his name—had a cup of ice chips that he was chewing on. He offered the cup to me. I was kind of grossed out by the idea of sharing the cup of ice with a stranger, but I was in no position to decline. I started chewing the ice and drank the melted water and consumed salt tabs while sitting there. I was smart enough this time to ensure that they were placed in the back pocket of my triathlon top. It was a savior. Another athlete also stopped to ask if there was anything she could do. I responded, "Please send an ambulance when spotted," to which she obliged and headed off. EMTs were readily available throughout the course, and ready to react to any given situation. Within ten minutes I could hear the sirens in the background and I knew they were headed towards me. I regained some focus and stood up. Surprisingly my senses had solidified and I actually felt pretty decent. The ten-minute hiatus was exactly what I needed. The additional hydration and salt were lifesavers.

Knowing that I had already traveled 127 miles thus far in the race, I calculated that I only had thirteen miles remaining and therefore decided I was not ready to quit. I started to walk and my legs felt rejuvenated. I feared that when the EMTs arrived they would deem me dehydrated and pull me from the race. I started to pick up my pace, looking back discreetly while hoping the race could continue and I would not be spotted. It felt devious yet comical, as if I had done something wrong and was covering for it. I actually laughed about the thought of this throughout the remaining thirteen miles. I was eager to share this new story with my family. I felt like I had beat the system! My journey towards completing my third full-distance Ironman would not be halted.

I crossed the finish line and enjoyed the glorious red carpet. I swear it never gets old. I soaked up the feeling of accomplishment at having earned the title again. After making my way back to the hotel and taking the most enjoyable hot shower, the heat easing my obviously over-exerted muscles, I awaited the taste of my victory at a local wine bar. We entered the winery and sat down with eager anticipation and ordered up a very expensive bottle to celebrate. My husband gave me the honors of having the first sip of the wine. I swirled my glass, smelled the aroma, and slowly sipped this intricate, complex drink when all of a sudden the first wave of nausea hit. Wait—this wasn't the plan. I was repulsed by the oaky, cigar- and black licorice-tasting wine. I was instantly revolted and within moments headed to the bathroom to pay the porcelain goddess a visit.

Ironman Arizona, on November 20, 2016, had since approached. It was a unique situation. The weather was extremely unpredictable, offering heat, rain, and sleet all in the same day. The wind was in your face and shifted throughout the entire race. People had pulled out from the race due to hypothermia. During transitions I found myself incapacitated; upon completion of the bike ride, I was unable to simply put my sneakers on and change into my dry, warm clothes that I'd packed in my transition bag with anticipation of weather concerns, which I'd identified the night prior. My fingers could not function. I apologized to the volunteer in utter embarrassment, asking her to help change me, tie my sneakers, and zip my jacket. I was also unable to put ChapStick on my weather-beaten lips. I hugged her as she wrapped the foil cover over my shoulders to help maintain heat and then I headed out to the course. I could tell every runner had been experiencing the same discomforts, as there were foil sheets littered everywhere throughout the course. Once I had completed the race and gathered my finisher medal and t-shirt, I vowed to myself that I would never compete in another long-distance race again. My kids reminded me that they had heard those words before.

In 2017 I decided to conquer Ironman Lake Placid, New York. This race was described as a badass with rolling hills and relentless climbs that would test some of the best riders and runners in the business. The allure of the beautiful, crisp Lake Placid swim seemed amazing and very inviting. The scenery of the wooded canvas of the course could not be matched. A four-hour drive to the venue seemed realistic and having the whole family in attendance would be a first. One week before the race, I had all of the bags carefully packed in order not to leave anything out. I reviewed the checklists multiple times and my eagerness to complete this course was palpable. I was careful to train with much more consideration during the few months leading up to the race. This course was going to be a challenge with all of the hill climbing. To properly prepare for this, every week on my way home from work I stopped by the local ski resort, parked my car, and did repetitive hill climbs. They were challenging to say the least but required in order to be successful. I felt more confident that my preparation would prove adequate and that my training was solid. I was ready and eager to test my abilities.

Three days before we were heading out to Lake Placid, my spirits were high and my adrenaline higher. My brother decided to host a pool party the weekend prior to leaving. The weather in July was typical for New England, hot and humid. Relaxing in a pool sounded like the ideal way to chill out with the family and talk about other things going on in the world. The kids were having a ball hanging out with their cousins and grandparents. The mood was very relaxed and enjoyable. As the kids did cannonballs and swan dives off the diving board, the adults sat back and basked in the heat. My son, next in line on the diving board, decided to display his creative leap into the water and he pranced his way over to the end of the diving board with a big smile on his face. He jumped up and down a few times on the springy board before unveiling his debut cannonball jump into the water, when he slipped and missed the edge of the board. At first I was unsure of what had happened. I heard an odd thump and then saw him hit the water. My gaze went to the end of the board where I noticed a clump of hair caught in the sandpaper-like texture. As he resurfaced I went into panic mode, worrying about an injury to his head. My mother instinct kicked in like a "spider sense" and without hesitation I dove into the water to ensure his safety. Within a couple of quick swim strokes I was holding his arms and asking as he flailed, "Are you ok? Are you bleeding?" to which he replied, "I am fine, Mom." He told me with a confident smile that he was not injured and at that exact moment—with the both of us flapping and treading water—the unforeseen happened. The most unimaginable, instant pain flooded my body. I realized that my right foot and my son's shin had collided. I could see stars. The pain had me holding back tears. As I made my way to the side of the pool and glanced down at my foot, I saw that my third toe was completely sideways. My husband and brother were considering relocating the toe but I feared something far worse than a dislocation.

Driving home from the medical clinic with X-rays in hand I was in awe and greatly disappointed. I had received confirmation of a clear break of my toe from the metatarsal bone. It was going to be six to eight weeks before life could resume as normal again. After all of the training that led to the race, it was clearly a disappointment. We still drove to Lake Placid, hoping that over the next three days my toe would magically heal and that I could fight through the discomfort. With all my gear still in the vehicle, we headed out. During the four-hour car ride, I had my toe elevated in the car next to the AC vent with hopes that it would help numb the pain and minimize the swelling. My determination to race was not going to be given up lightly.

Upon entering the Ironman village, I was desperate enough to purchase sneakers that were developed to help folks with injuries. I marched around the village hiding my dismay, unwilling to admit defeat. My stepson Bryant and I decided to take our bikes out on the course and test my ability to ride. This would be a good opportunity to understand what my foot would feel like during the race. I lightly cranked my bike shoe securely, clipped in to the bike pedals, and off we went. Approximately a quarter mile into the ride, I was done. The excruciating pain could not be tolerated. Biking 112 miles and then running a full marathon could be more detrimental to recovery. The risk could impair healing and compromise my next race set for Louisville, Kentucky, in the fall. We decided to be supportive spectators to all those that raced Lake Placid that year. This was my opportunity to cheer on fellow athletes, but my displeasure was obviously evident.

As I have gathered from lots of endurance athletes' stories: The longer you stay competitive, the higher is the likelihood that there will be events that can alter your planned course. Since this outcome, I realized maybe bubble wrap and self-isolation are the only ways to avoid injury the week prior to a race.

In 2017 I ventured to a new race venue: Louisville, Kentucky, on October 15. My fastest Ironman to date. I broke the thirteen-hour time. To think it was only three years from the beginning of this journey, when I was struggling to complete the race in seventeen hours, to finishing in just under thirteen hours. Four hours faster than the first time I decided to sport my presence. I really considered my progression to be self-satisfying.

My final race of the year was Tempe, Arizona November, 19, 2017. It was my third and final time racing the beautiful Tempe course. At this point I was very familiar with the race layout, and it had become less intimidating. This race was unusually unique for me. Being a New Englander I rarely see any unusual animals roaming the area. Occasionally you could spot a bear or a moose but other than that not much stirs too much attention. This race was exciting, during the bike ride I was able to spot a rather large rattle snake on the ledge of the road, and it was playing roulette with its life considering all of the near-by bicyclists in the area. I would like to tell a fish story that the snake was 10 feet long, but rather it was medium sized and coiled up with it rattle clearly present. That being said it was one of the unusual highlights of the race.

After such a great year, I decided to set my goals for Ironman Kona World Championships. This would be the ultimate goal. All of these Ironman races would make me worthy of sporting my presence. I had sacrificed so much over the years, and Kona would be my reward. My sights were set. The countdown was on. All that said, the race in Tempe was beautiful and the completion marked another race closer to earning my ticket to the World Championships. As the year finished up, my goals were met and I was for sure improving. It would be a year to remember; my goals and objectives had been achieved and the results exceeded my expectations.

In 2018 I met another goal of mine: running the Boston Marathon on April 16. This had always been a dream of mine. Running the course five years after the Marathon bombings felt very surreal. I considered this race a celebration of overcoming tragedy. We were all united and the catastrophe that happened in 2013 would not break the spirit of the nation. This race brought some of the most elite runners in the entire world and it was an opportunity to celebrate a sport that unifies athletes towards a common goal.

Of course, this year hosted one of the most difficult race conditions the Boston Marathon had seen in decades. The temperature was in the thirties and there were wind gusts of up to forty-five miles per hour. It rained and even hailed at times. It was both physically and mentally challenging. I felt for my family who awaited my arrival at the finish line. They enthusiastically waited amongst the other spectators in the terrible weather conditions.

I started the race strong and feeling good, although I was uncomfortable throughout the day due to the temperature and rain. My sneakers were covered in mud from all of the walking through the fields just to get to the starting line. I didn't care what the conditions were, I had waited for this moment for years. Nothing could deflate my eagerness to take on the course. As I approached the starting line, my adrenaline spiked and off I went with 26.2 miles of pure enjoyment ahead. I embraced the entire day. At approximately ten miles into the run, my fingers were feeling the bite of the cold and were drenched. I made the decision to ditch my wet gloves and retreat my hands into my jacket. Miles later I realized that the added wind protection offered by the wet gloves was required and that I had made a big mistake in shedding them. Around mile eighteen there was a spectator who had a bin full of used socks. She yelled out to the runners that they were available for the taking. I willingly surged at the opportunity to grab a pair. The socks weren't the most pristine-looking and while it was concerning not knowing the journey they had taken prior to being placed on my hands, they were my savior. I was so grateful for the kindness that the Boston community offered. Nearing the end of the race, I was amazed to spot my family in the stadium seating. I waved and smiled as I crossed the finish line of the Boston Marathon with a moderate time of 4:40:11. Given the conditions, I was thrilled to be blessed with the ability to embrace this as it truly was a once-in-a-lifetime opportunity.

When choosing an Ironman race, you have to consider that the venues generally fill up very fast. I had registered for Ironman Texas on April 28, 2018, a whole year in advance not realizing I would also have the opportunity to run the Boston Marathon. I could not pass on either opportunity, regardless of them being only two weeks apart. I had defined my plan to qualify for Kona and did not want to forgo either race. They were both too important to me. That meant that a week and a half after completing Boston, I would be flying to Texas to compete in the Ironman.

The Texas course had since changed from prior years. In Texas 2015, the race through The Woodlands offered some very scenic routes that encompassed shaded country roads along with open fields. The new course was fast and flat with little to no shade to retreat under. The majority of the bike ride was on a highway. Course officials were limited due to the safety on the new course design. The swim was similar to previous years, and I was comfortable going into it knowing that I had conquered this portion before. The bike ride was daunting. It was unusual to be riding on a highway, but the course offered protection from the vehicles as they were blocked off. I was nervous thinking about biking in this setting, but surprisingly it was fun and seemed quicker than other courses I had ridden in the past. It was a hot day and I was eager to get off the bike. I proceeded to the run and couldn't wait to check this race off. As the sun was setting and the course was nearing completion, I was excited to be reunited with my husband at the finish line. Ironman number seven was complete with five more to go. As we walked back to the parking garage, I noticed that I was starting to get light-headed. I grasped my husband's arm tighter, before releasing and completely collapsing on the road directly in front of the parking garage. I could not take another step. My husband barked at me to get up. This was not safe. At that point across the road there was a lineup of black limos. I was aware that at this particular race the Prince of Bahrain was present. Post-race the Prince's entourage was awaiting his arrival. The men quickly ran over to us, offering assistance while my husband could seek medical help. I was beside myself, embarrassed to no end. The Prince's team offered their assistance as I preferred the idea of hiding in utter humiliation. If you are going to pass out and make a scene, why not make it dramatic?

I also recommitted to tackling Lake Placid on July 22, 2018. It was going to be redemption from the previous year which had been deflating. But this was a new opportunity to confront the course that I had been eagerly awaiting. I purchased a new bike (an aerodynamic, hot-pink beauty which I named "Blue," just because). Blue was a great bike except that she had challenged me earlier in the season. I had had her professionally fitted and decided to test her out on an Olympic-distance triathlon. During the bike portion of the race, I noticed that my aerodynamic position seemed to be shifting; the handlebars started to drop and the cockpit was slowly descending during the first two miles of the twenty-mile ride. The mechanics had missed the opportunity to tighten up the aerobars. I finished the race looking rather odd as I was basically sitting on top of the front wheel—but hey, as always, I got it done. I was concerned of a repeat performance, but the bike shop apologized and had since fixed the problem.

As Lake Placid played out, I can confirm from my perspective that the course was challenging but also one of the loveliest venues out there. The swim was unusual for me. Normally I get a little flustered with what's to come with all the commotion in the water, but Lake Placid was rather calming. Weeks prior to the race lots of funny stories, based on the movies, surfaced regarding a crocodile-style monster living in the lake, but those thoughts didn't consume me race morning. Instead it was very enjoyable. The water was crystal clear and there was a line under the water that was so visible it allowed me to use it as course guidance to ensure I was staying on track, making the swim a calm part of the race for me. The bike ride was one of the most difficult yet rewarding rides I have ever been on. The course took you through some very challenging climbs, yet the downhill reward made up for the grit climbing them. Visually the course was spectacular; passing lakes, ski resorts, biking up and down the mountains—it was truly an event. The run didn't offer much relief as the climbs and descents didn't let up, but the spectators were amazing, constantly offering words of encouragement and maintaining a very high level of excitement. Upon completing the race, the red carpet at the finish line was exhilarating. The turnout of spectators ended up being one of the best in the Ironman circuit, and the encouragement throughout the course was a highlight. I will never forget that race.

The last race of 2018 was Ironman Chattanooga, Tennessee, on September 30. What a fun venue, and getting to snack on Little Debbies guilt-free after race day was a treat. This race was the first time that I would experience a canceled swim. Horrible flooding in the area had made the water quality unsafe for swimmers. At first I was upset since running an Ironman meant competing in all three events, but as this wasn't my first rodeo, my disappointment was manageable. Waking up an hour later ended up being a delight and the idea of not plunging myself into cold water at 7 a.m. wasn't all that bad. Plus, the course offered an extra four miles of biking which would have made this course even longer than the typical Ironman event.

This year I had also embraced a new nutrition routine. It was a powder mix that you added water to, and it would take out the complexity of consuming nutrition approximately every fifteen minutes while also having to maintain the proper fluid and salt levels. The mixture would supply me with all the carbohydrates, salts, and proteins required for the bike ride and run, based on my nutritional needs as identified throughout training. I would not need to consume any course products, making it simpler for me to control my nutrition and salt intake. My plan required me to drink one bottle of water with the powder mixture every hour. Therefore, I placed three bottles on my bike which would last me for three hours of the race. I also put another three bottles inside my special needs bag, which I would only have access to once during the bike ride at mile fifty-six. The special needs stop would supply me with the required nutrition for the remainder of the bike race.

Feeling primed and ready to go, the race started. I felt stronger than normal. Maybe it was the cancellation of the swim that made me more vibrant going straight to the bike. As the race progressed, I continually monitored my racing pace which was very fast for me. I was comfortably biking 18.5 miles per hour and noticed that I wasn't being passed. I could see the riders' age on their calves so I watched for ladies in my age group to pass but I wasn't spotting too many. This definitely stroked my ego. Granted, I had started the ride as one of the earlier riders as we were allowed to enter the bike course per our bib numbers. My number was 458 out of 3,000 competitors. So I had a good head start.

As the miles clicked off I was getting close to the fifty-six-mile area, and I could hear that rackety cowbell calling my name. I looked up and was so excited to see my husband yelling "Stacy!" It is always so invigorating seeing a loved one. I felt so supported. My husband was repeatedly yelling in my direction, "Stacy, you're in the lead." I smiled to myself and chanted "WOOP WOOP!!" That was just what I needed to hear. He was pointing ahead and I felt the extra adrenaline kick in. I knew he had a good idea of my position and placement since we had trackers on us; as we ride over the GPS placemats, the tracker gives updates with an idea of pace and position along with estimated completion time. *I am a badass, life is good.*

The extra kick pushed me to increase my bike speed. Not a good thing. There was a lot of the race left. Endurance races are all about pace, and any extra assertion would likely bite me in the future. At that point I was clipping almost nineteen miles per hour. I was getting concerned as I was almost out of my nutrition drink, and I was now at mile fifty-eight with no special needs in sight. I started pinging riders in my view as to inquire when the special needs would appear. Some were unaware as they probably had no reason to utilize them in the first place. Finally one gentleman acknowledged me and stated, "We passed it already. Didn't you see all the folks near the downtown bend?" Special needs was over there? Oy! What now? I was out of nutrition and five miles past special needs. Do I go backwards? That would be dangerous with all the riders in the area. I had to plug forward and wait six more miles until the next aid station where I would need to consume course nutrition from that point on.

I had only trained this year using the powdered formula. The idea of course gels (which have a pineapple flavor), Gatorades, and other snacks did not fare well with me. But I had no choice, this was my unchosen destiny. After finishing the bike ride, having consumed food that did not sit well, I was already in a foul mood. My race was compromised, but not finishing what I had started was never going to be an option. I greeted my husband at 116 miles, unclipped my bike shoes, handed my bike over to a volunteer, and walked towards T2. In dismay I spoke with my husband who said, “Couldn’t you hear me? I was screaming at you and pointing across the road stating ‘Stacy, SPECIAL NEEDS!!’” As I pondered what I thought I’d heard him say, I realized “YOU’RE IN THE LEAD” was not necessarily a true statement. *Oh my goodness*, I was so focused on finding him and sharing a smile and blowing a kiss. Daniel had been destroyed knowing that I’d just blown past my planned course nutrition for the remainder of the race. Heading into T2, I was concerned that I had started the race with my powdered formula, then converted to course nutrition, and I was now back in transition going to use the powdered nutrition again for the run. I was definitely worried about what all these changes would have in store for me.

Months earlier I had purchased a CamelBak backpack, designed with a fluid reservoir. The evening before the race, I poured in a concentrated amount of powder that would allow me to run two and a half hours before needing a refill at the run special needs stop. The powder consumed half of the backpack bladder. Concerned that the backpack could leak while in my transition bag, I decided to add two bottles of water prior to taking off on the run. All was good and back on plan. I zipped up the bag, clicked together the chest fasteners, and off I went. When exiting the transition tent, I decided it would be a good idea to take some hydration. Sucking on the straw, I was pulling up powder through the plastic tube. My straw was jammed. The water would not be able to mix with the powder. I tried jiggling the backpack while growing even more infuriated. The backpack was heavy and I was damned to be carrying it on my back while being unusable. Tears started to stream down my face as my frustration only continued to build. I spotted my husband less than a quarter mile up. I stopped to give him a quick update and I explained to him my dilemma. I tried to shake the bag but the jam was so backed up, making the hydration pack unusable. I unclicked the fasteners and hooked it by a nearby trash can, grumbling to myself, *Screw it*. My husband pleaded for me to pick it up, almost demanding. "Take a minute, open it up," he said, "and try to resolve the jam." I was in no mood for this. I was already starting to have stomach pains. I wanted to complete the course and move on. My husband grew irritated and tried to coerce me to go back and pick up the backpack. He knew that I was not allowed course help from anyone other than a volunteer, and he was therefore unable to grab it for me. If he helped me I could risk being disqualified from the race. He stared at the backpack on the ground in utter dismay as I trotted off onto the course.

The first mile rolled around and I mumbled to myself, *Boy am I screwed, I knew it*. What the hell was I thinking? Did I really toss away all of my nutrition? My special needs bag had additional packets of powder and water to be added halfway through the race, and I had no way of utilizing them. I had thrown a full-fledged hissy hit and had no one to blame but myself.

I hit the first aid station and browsed my food options like at a Costco. The mere thought of more gels, bananas, cola, and fruit slices made my stomach hurt. I grabbed a few products and stuffed them in my pockets and headed off. As soon as I had some of the gel I grew sick, my stomach churned and retaliated. I assumed the race was over. I couldn't fight the nausea any longer. Over the next few miles of walking and hurling, my stomach eased up. It settled. The mixture of oddities had been purged and from that point on I decided to stick to Gatorade and bananas for the remainder of the race. It worked and I would not deviate from this new nutrition plan. Twelve hours and thirty-eight minutes later the race was complete. A finisher medal was placed around my neck and I was that much closer to the Ironman World Championships. The thought of making it to the Holy Grail of triathlons was that much sweeter. I had endured so much to date, I deserved this opportunity.

Goal in Sight

As 2019 rolled in, I had signed up for my last three Ironman events with the hope of clinching my World Championship ticket. First up was Santa Rosa, California. After all of the devastating wildfires that the Napa region had suffered, this was a very surreal moment. Homes were destroyed and the thought of seeing people living in trailers while they awaited their homes being rebuilt was heart-wrenching. The damage to the beautiful land and vineyards was almost too much to comprehend.

While biking throughout the 112-mile course on race day I suffered minor headaches, but I was able to keep the pain manageable. This became a common theme during training and I got used to it as it felt routine. With the stress of working a full-time job, taking care of the family, and training, I shrugged it off as a sign of coping with the stress.

Four weeks after the completion of Santa Rosa, I was toeing the starting line of Boulder, Colorado. With the limited acclimation to the higher elevation of the race course, I found that this race proved more challenging than originally anticipated. Granted, it was a very beautiful setting for a race, but I struggled throughout. This wasn't considered one of the easier venues and I could feel the challenge taking an immense toll on my physical being. During the race I didn't feel like myself. As a repeat of Santa Rosa, my head hurt and my body was fatigued. I saw my husband and friends throughout the race and relayed my dismay over my performance. It had only been a month since Santa Rosa and I clearly knew that this was not enough time to heal and recover, but my goals were to complete twelve races this year. So I pushed through the negative thoughts and completed with a respectable time in my eyes. Not the most impressive, but nothing to be ashamed of either. After flying home from Colorado, I had to take time to heal. My body was telling me that I was being too taxing on it.

My family has always enjoyed scuba diving together, and we have traveled the world seeking new locations to explore the oceans and the creatures that occupy them. This hobby has also carried over into owning an aquarium. This allows us to share the same enjoyment in our living room as underwater. One of my husband's passions is creating a beautiful saltwater tank in our home. He takes pride in his personal seascape and enjoys filling it with exotic fish and coral. Every year we venture to a coral show in New Jersey to pick out new coral pieces to embellish the tank with. In 2019, the event occurred two weeks after the Boulder Ironman. I was feeling good and rested, and I welcomed the idea of any conversations that didn't revolve around triathlons. It would be a well-needed physical and mental break from the sport. The coral show was a two-day event which hosted hundreds of vendors and we would wander from each person's station to view their displays of prized pieces available for purchase. It was pleasing to the eye and an enjoyable way to spend the day.

The doors opened early Saturday morning to welcome the season. We rushed into the show with a cooler in hand to place any coral pieces that we purchased. Each coral we eyed up came with a unique name, like Jelly Bean frags, Cornbred pieces, and a multitude of variations of soft corals, brain corals, torches, and SPSs. Each piece was unique in color and formation and it was enjoyable to have conversations with vendors to understand what they were selling and what environment the piece would thrive in. Whether it be a high-light area or a low water flow, each piece needed its own optimal surroundings to flourish. My husband was all too eager to wedge himself in between excitable visitors which made me smile. He was delighted by the experience every year. I stood back five feet allowing my husband to bask at all the beautiful coral. It was enjoyable seeing how delighted he was with eagerness to purchase new pieces. I tried to sneak a peek over the shoulders of strangers every now and then so that my husband could share his likes and dislikes. An hour into the show I snuck over to my husband; something was wrong. My eyes started to swirl, my head felt like it had been hit by a hammer, and the overzealous feeling of nausea came over me. Feeling devastated by all the support my husband has given me over the years, this was my time to support him with his passions. There was no way I was going to have him miss this event. He had eagerly awaited it for months—he even purchased VIP tickets to allow us access to the vendors an hour before the general population. I grabbed my husband's arm and whispered that I was not feeling well and was almost at the point of passing out. I reassured him that I was OK, but I was going to head across the street to the hotel. He agreed but was concerned. I again reassured him I was fine but needed to lie down to rest for a bit.

Begging the chef at the hotel restaurant for some ice for my sweltering headache, the gentleman must have noticed my distress as he was so prompt in getting me a large, clear bag of ice chunks that was leaking from the corner. I thanked him for his ability to work so quickly. He clearly was able to see the pain in my eyes. I made my way back to the hotel room, turned off the lights, and plopped the bag of ice on my head. Lying there I started to feel the pressure ease. It was all very odd. Within an hour I felt like a new person. The pain and suffering had subsided and had passed as quickly as it came on. Oddly enough I felt OK and headed back to the coral show, excited to see my husband and willing to support his passions for the remainder of the weekend.

On September 8, 2019, I ran my twelfth full-distance Ironman in Madison, Wisconsin. This race was pivotal in my triathlon career. It was my opportunity to earn my ticket to the Ironman World Championship in Kona, Hawaii. My goals were coming to fruition. I had to complete this race in order to submit my ticket and seize my spot. Hoping that nothing would go wrong, I couldn't be more excited for this day. I had learned so much over the last eleven races and had improved immensely, taking almost four and a half hours off my race times since my first Ironman in Texas 2015. I couldn't be more elated. I had overcome so many obstacles. I realized that setting goals and remaining passionate about the sport had brought me to this moment.

I was feeling amazing, excited, and confident. Everything was executed as planned. The swim through Lake Monona was refreshing and challenging and the bike ride went perfectly. The bike course was beautiful and scenic and the crowds of people throughout were electric. I had no issues during the ride and the 26.2-mile run was a celebration that I will never forget. We ran through Camp

Randall Stadium which was a welcomed treat, and past the Capitol in Downtown Wisconsin. I had a smile from ear to ear as every single mile checked off during the marathon was just one step closer to my overall goal. My mental state was strong, and not one negative thought crossed my mind throughout the entire day.

I ran down the finishing red carpet and could celebrate joyfully. The feeling of completion has never subsided with any race. Each time you complete this journey and cross the finish line is an indescribable feeling of accomplishment that will never get old. The finish chute is a celebration between you, your fellow athletes, family and friends, and even people you have never met before. Thousands of people are there celebrating your victories. It's one of the few times in my life when I have really felt on top of the world. I was so relieved and I was the happiest I have been in my entire triathlon career. I was beaming with pride and looking towards my family and friends, enjoying every moment that came with this celebration of a very long, monumental triathlon career. There was nothing more important to celebrate at that moment.

The day couldn't have gone any better. Fabulous weather. Amazing course. I planned to celebrate in the evening with my family and to enjoy every single moment. I had completed my mission. Twelve full-distance Ironmans had been accomplished, and I had clinched my legacy ticket to get to the World Championship! This was a historic moment in my life, one never to be forgotten. I had worked as hard as any athlete competing in any race, but this one was the cherry on top of the cake. I still can’t let this moment go. I hope to remember every single smile that went into this race. It was the highlight of my triathlon journey.

Not Created Equal

One month after the completion of the race in Madison, Wisconsin, I wasn't feeling well. I noticed at work that simple tasks had become very difficult. Writing sentences had become unclear and tough. I would look at what I had written over and over and things just weren't making sense; it was incoherent. I was confused. I brushed these insecurities off and just assumed that I was a forty-four-year-old woman. I put it down to age and its natural progression. I had also started struggling with daily headaches. Every evening after I drove home from work I had to take a nap to give my tired, fatigued head some well-needed rest. Sometimes I didn't sleep but I felt as though I required this decompression. It helped me continue through the evening feeling a little better and being ready to return to work the next morning. I had had some time off from running since the last triathlon, and I was feeling physically good. I entered into a recovery mode and had decided to start running small distances of one to two miles a day, a couple of days a week. I felt good and mechanically my body felt as though it was healing nicely. There were no issues in my knees, hip, back, or feet, except that my right leg seemed to have become slightly weaker and my stride offered a new drag in my running gait. I figured that maybe there was a muscle imbalance developing but otherwise mechanically everything else felt fine.

November came and went, and although my symptoms had not improved, they also hadn't gotten worse. It had been a month of running. One evening after a run I decided to look at the bottom of my sneakers and noticed that the right sole of my sneaker was worn down unevenly compared to my left. It seemed odd but it also explained the obvious drag while running. Once again, I attributed this to all of the prep work I'd done over the course of the year to become ready for my final twelfth 140.6 race of the year.

November 28th, 2019, was a monumental day for me. Completing twelve full-distance 140.6 races had qualified me for the Holy Grail of triathlons in Hawaii. At noon eastern, I was allowed to submit my ticket to qualify for this classic event. With eager anticipation and my family standing over me, we hit submit on my application. My hands were trembling from the excitement. The journey had been very long and arduous to get to this point. After submitting all of the documents to prove that I had sufficiently completed the prerequisites to allow me to participate, the waiting part began. Now that my application had been submitted, I eagerly awaited my acceptance letter from Ironman. If approved, it would be granted in February 2020. *Let the waiting game begin.* It felt like it would take an eternity, but my reward would be forthcoming.

By December I had noticed that my speech had become slightly impaired and retrieving a word was a new struggle. At this point, a month had gone by and I felt it necessary to speak to my primary care physician regarding my symptoms. I had an appointment scheduled for the first week of December to discuss my concerns. As any doctor would, they sent me for a battery of tests that included checking for vitamin deficiencies and concerns such as Lyme disease. I felt hopeful since Lyme disease replicates some of the symptoms I had been suffering from. Within two days all of the tests came back negative. I called my doctor who scheduled an MRI. On December 13, 2019—my forty-fifth birthday—I lay on the imaging machine with tears streaming down my cheeks. I knew something was painfully wrong. Until that point, I had been reluctant to share my concerns with my children and family. Only my husband and mother were aware of my concerns, as I chose not to alarm anyone else with what could be a simple progression of age—or at least this was my way of coping or not coping with what was to come. My online research had pointed to something in my brain as I could easily check off multiple symptoms of concern.

The evening of December 13th, as I headed home from the hospital, my family was on their way over to celebrate my birthday. I entered my home after the test to eagerly greet my children. The house was filled with balloons and the typical excitement of waiting for the rest of my family to arrive in order to start the celebration. As I walked through the door, my cell phone started ringing. Instantly, I went pale. I knew what was coming. I had done my research and was pretty sure something was not right. My doctor informed me that something was very wrong, and I needed to go directly to the hospital and meet with a neurosurgeon immediately. I was recommended to pack a bag and head on over. I quietly went into my bedroom listening to the doctor on the phone, contemplating how to tell my family in the other room. Walking out of my bedroom was one of the hardest things I have ever had to do. My children instantly knew something was terribly wrong. I explained to my children that I needed to pack a bag and head to the hospital. I then had to call my family and cancel the celebration that was about to take place within the hour. It was the most painful conversation; no one can prepare you for this kind of blow in such an insensitive way over the phone. Describing briefly that there was a concern with my brain and not actually knowing the ramifications of what was next was indescribable. My parting words to my family were to please take care of our children while we head to the hospital to meet with the neurosurgeon.

Nothing can prepare anyone to share that kind of news with children who have no idea anything is wrong in the first place. My family felt betrayed because I had not shared my symptoms or concerns with them. Maybe it was selfish, but as a mom, I felt that I needed to be a protector. My job is to be strong and hold the fort down. Weakness is a feeling that I almost always suppress so that we can function as a strong family. Everyone in my family was taken off guard that day, and till this day I am still guilt-ridden.

We packed my luggage and headed to the hospital without any sense of what was to come. After a long night, we met with the neurosurgeon who took further tests to understand the full capacity of what was going on within my brain. In the early morning, the neurosurgeon visited us again. He explained to me that I had a five-centimeter tumor on my brain—known as an AVM—that had been hemorrhaging multiple times throughout the year and had since ruptured. The intense feeling I experienced during the coral show was likely one of the hemorrhaging events. An AVM, which stands for arteriovenous malformation, is an abnormal tangle of blood vessels. These blood vessels connect to the arteries in the brain. The arteries take oxygen-rich blood from the heart to the brain and AVMs are known to disrupt this process. The cause of this is still unknown and over time it can lead to serious brain damage.

Less than 1 percent of the human population have them which makes an AVM a very rare disease. This all explained why I dealt with ongoing headaches, was unable to write coherent sentences, and had a lack of muscle tone on my right side. I was going to be rushed into surgery that week. The surgeon explained to me that I would be wide-awake during this craniotomy. The reason behind being awake was so that I could communicate with the surgeons if something were to go wrong during the surgery. The surgery was to take about six hours in which I would be awake for over half of it. With much apprehension, I was not very keen on the idea of being awake. However, the surgeon reaffirmed that it was very important that I communicate to ensure that the delicate surgery wasn't doing damage to surrounding areas that could cause long-term effects. Post-surgery I would have a titanium plate mounted to my skull.

A few days after the surgery was complete I was pleasantly surprised to remember each of the conversations I had had with the staff during surgery. It was almost kind of comical—at times. One of the surgeons noticed the M-Dot tattoo on the back of my calf and was intrigued about my experiences. Other conversations revolved around my favorite dinners, to which I was trying to respond that "I love steak," but the surgeon continually asked me, "Why do you like to eat snakes?" I remember laughing during surgery and saying, "What is wrong with these people, I love steak—you know, 'moo moo.'"

Surprisingly, being awake during a surgery was not painful. The brain itself has no pain receptors, and so recovery wasn't as bad as expected. The headaches were probably the most difficult to deal with. My writing was still lacking at times, and I was still feeling discouraged, but the doctor told me that they were convinced I would make a good recovery, which could take up to a year. Physical therapy, occupational therapy, and speech therapy were some of the treatments I would need to participate in to ensure a good recovery.

My family, extended family, friends, and coworkers were my rock through all of this. My loving parents, husband, kids, and brother were constantly by my side. They frequently visited and called to check up. I am beyond blessed to have felt so supported.

Three days after surgery, while lying in my bed, I was abruptly alerted to the fact that my right arm, tongue, and right side of my lips were numbing and tingling. I didn't know what was happening to me, but talking to my neurologist I discovered that I was suffering my first seizure. This was alarming to me, not understanding what this was all about. When I think of seizures I think of blacking out and the inability to control your movements, but mine were focal and affected only the right side of my body. As the weeks progressed, I started to develop seizures regularly, two to three times a day. My medication was making me irritated, agitated, and very sad. Therefore, I was in the process of discovering new medication that might help my situation. These changes were a process of trial and error with hopes to having a suitable solution to help minimize future episodes.

At times I found myself severely depressed, for multiple reasons. I've always been an active person, working out five to six days a week, sometimes twice a day, and now this was no longer an option in my life. I always enjoyed work and, at this time, I was unable to form legible and intelligible writing. My family had to deal with my agitation, which made me additionally upset. I dealt with many post-surgery nightmares, which were extremely vivid. Sleep between headaches, therefore, was difficult, inhibiting my rest and recovery. Worst of all, I was unable to drive. Massachusetts laws prevent you from driving six months from your last seizure. I felt helpless.

Recovery

Three months post-surgery I was starting to come around and enjoy walking and being with family when the unfortunate events occurred all over the world. The Coronavirus (COVID-19) outbreak had made its way into the United States. The realization that the country must stay in self-isolation to prevent the virus from spreading just created another level of depression. Surprisingly, my daughter Bailey returned from college early, my son was required to finish his high-school education from home, and my husband had to work from home as well. With all of these changes occurring I actually feel surprisingly blessed. I am surrounded by my family. At times we all get a little stir-crazy and cranky being in the same home twenty-four hours a day but it works. We are lucky. We have the opportunity to spend time together, play games, and embrace each other's company. After the last five years of competing, this retreat allows me to really reconnect with everyone. This circumstance is temporarily inconvenient but I get to reap the rewards of enjoying what has been the most important aspect of my life and reconnecting with what really defines who I am: my family.

Not knowing what my future would look like deepened my depression. On November 28, 2019, I had received my golden ticket to compete in the World Championships. With my new diagnosis, my doctor would not confirm nor deny if the endurance training contributed to my medical condition. Therefore, I am at a crossroads to discover whether or not competing could hinder my health further. Post-surgery, I was given another MRI to see whether the swelling and blood residue on my brain was starting to heal. This led to the discovery of another AVM which was located on the right lobe of my brain. Although this cyst is small in nature, I am scared of a possible future surgery. The right-lobe system affects different parts of your body, unlike the left side. If this cyst continues to grow, I could suffer vision and balance issues, among other ailments. And so I am left with trying to evaluate what is important to me in life. I never want to put my husband, children, or family through this kind of pain again. I have been a fortunate woman all these years, but as fate has it, I am at a crossroads when it comes to my future endeavors. I am appreciative of everything I have accomplished over the years. Racing twelve full-distance Ironman races is an achievement. So I try not to dwell on my unfortunate mishaps to date; they are a part of my story, my life, and my legacy. Therefore, I must walk delicately with a new future vision of how life may look.

Deciding my path forward, I awaited my acceptance to the World Championship triathlon. I was unsure if this was a path that I was willing to take, if it was even safe enough to continue. There is a lot of training that goes into preparing yourself for this great challenge. Not knowing whether or not my second AVM cyst will continue to grow and create another hemorrhage on the brain creates serious doubt over whether the challenge is worth the reward.

I was contemplating whether or not I could even put my family through the stress of watching the Kona triathlon, not knowing where I am on the swim course, the bike course, or the run. It would be terrifying, and I would be greedy to put them through the torture, pain, and concern for my health. I also feel that I worked so hard for this incredible reward and that I deserve the taste of victory. I am saddened over how this journey has come to an end. I sit at home and recover and look at my treadmill, my bike which now rests on the trainer, my medals of achievements and cannot understand why all this has been taken from me at this point in my athletic career. I feel as though life is unfair, and people don't understand the sacrifices I've made over the last six years to get to this point. To have it all taken away from me at the final steps of finishing my journey as a triathlete is a pain beyond description. People remind me to relish in all of my accomplishments, but yet I feel defeated.

In February 2020 I found out that I had been accepted to compete in the Ironman Kona World Championship to take place on October 10, 2020. This was a bittersweet moment. I had waited close to a decade for this. I had sacrificed so much of my life to get to this point. I hate that I resent myself for this feeling. I earned this moment and now it is being stolen from me. Friends and family remind me to be grateful for all of my accomplishments, yet I am depressed, angry, and feeling sorry for myself. How can this be? I am so self-centered, is all I can think.

I have since decided that my triathlon journey has to come to an end. I have put up my bike for sale. I have sold all of my triathlon gear, including helmets, wetsuits, bike glasses, etc. This year has been far too painful. I need to refocus and relish in the accomplishments over the last six years of my life and reward myself with the knowledge of all that I've accomplished. Going forward, I'll need to focus on all of my memories, the friends I've met, and the stories that built my legacy in the triathlon world. This is the time to stop feeling sorry for myself. I am a survivor. In creating a new life, I have to create a new me. How does one accomplish that?

I have decided I need to rebuild a new life and make new memories. I need my family and children to feel secure that I am not going anywhere. I choose life, and the ability to see my children grow up and someday have families of their own. I have reevaluated what is important to me. Not knowing where my life will take me, I have decided that sharing my story in writing this book is my way of finding the new me. In my journey, and in life in general, sometimes we do not know the path for which we are headed. Reinventing our journey is important when realizing that life takes different paths and turns, and that this is not a failure. It is exciting to come up with a new plan for what my next journey will become. Whether it will be writing, enjoying yoga, or going for a hike, I will find a new way to enjoy my life.

My message to all readers is that life should be appreciated, celebrated, and never taken for granted. We must enjoy the journey each one of us takes as there are no guarantees in life. For some life can be short, while others get a longer journey. Feel blessed no matter the life you've been given. Change is inevitable, which is why you must learn to embrace all of it. Never stop looking for ways to reinvent yourself. Feeling sorry and angry for the things we can't control is not productive to leading a healthy, positive life. As I figure out my new life, I will remember all of the amazing things I have done up until this point. Going forward, I will establish all of the amazing things that are ahead of me. This story is about change and embracing the things we cannot control. I am blessed for everything that has been given to me, and I shall not feel sorry for myself any longer for the changes that I am experiencing at this time. I must remain positive and be open to new and exciting challenges—whatever they may be.

As I navigate these uncharted territories, I remind myself that I am surrounded by my husband, children, parents, and friends. And as I continue my recovery, I remain grateful for everything that has made me who I am. I am not a quitter, and my journey does not stop here. My future adventures may be limited to my capabilities, but my desire to achieve greatness has never subsided. As I continue to develop new interests, I remind myself never to despair over my conditions. I am not defined by my limitations. Instead I will focus on my aspirations to be a better me. Life is short; embrace the beauty of it. Relish in the idea that you can aspire to be the best you. Never lose sight of a goal. Life may need to be modified according to its plan, but that doesn't mean you need to limit your ability to achieve greatness.

Ultimately, I remind myself that I am lucky. I am a survivor. My legacy is a reminder of where I have come from. My future is wide open to new possibilities. Every day I contemplate what's to come. This is new to me since my path was always predefined. I had a goal and I pursued it and I conquered it. Now is my opportunity to set forward and charter new territories, whatever they may be. I am inspired by what's to come and feel optimistic regarding life. I honor my abilities while acknowledging my limitations. I will continue to be open to the new challenges ahead and embrace the fact that the sky is the limit.

ACKNOWLEDGEMENTS

To my favorite people in the world, my husband Daniel and three amazing kids Bryant, Bailey and Kyle who never stopped believing in me or my passion.

My loving parents and brother: Karen, Tony, Millie & Tony

My dearest friends & colleagues: Kathy, Lisa, Eric, Colleen, Mel & Ashley

Life's greatest journeys are inspired by personal accomplishments, rewards, challenges & triumphs, and are best celebrated with friends and family.

Printed in Great Britain
by Amazon